# JEWISH WITH FEELING

RIVERHEAD BOOKS

*a member of*

Penguin Group (USA) Inc.

New York

2005

# JEWISH WITH FEELING

## A GUIDE TO MEANINGFUL JEWISH PRACTICE

RABBI ZALMAN SCHACHTER-SHALOMI

with JOEL SEGEL

RIVERHEAD BOOKS

Published by the Penguin Group

Penguin Group (USA) Inc., 375 Hudson Street, New York, New York 10014, USA •
Penguin Group (Canada), 10 Alcorn Avenue, Toronto, Ontario, Canada M4V 3B2 (a division of
Pearson Penguin Canada Inc.) • Penguin Books Ltd, 80 Strand, London WC2R 0RL,
England • Penguin Ireland, 25 St Stephen's Green, Dublin 2, Ireland (a division of Penguin
Books Ltd) • Penguin Group (Australia), 250 Camberwell Road, Camberwell, Victoria 3124,
Australia (a division of Pearson Australia Group Pty Ltd) • Penguin Books India Pvt Ltd,
11 Community Centre, Panchsheel Park, New Delhi–110 017, India • Penguin Group (NZ),
Cnr Airborne and Rosedale Roads, Albany, Auckland 1310, New Zealand (a division of Pearson
New Zealand Ltd) • Penguin Books (South Africa) (Pty) Ltd, 24 Sturdee Avenue, Rosebank,
Johannesburg 2196, South Africa

Penguin Books Ltd, Registered Offices: 80 Strand, London WC2R 0RL, England

Library of Congress Cataloging-in-Publication Data

Schachter-Shalomi, Zalman, date.
Jewish with feeling: a guide to meaningful Jewish practice /
Zalman Schachter-Shalomi with Joel Segel.
p.   cm.
Includes bibliographical references.
ISBN 1-57322-280-1
1. Judaism.   I. Segel, Joel.   II. Title.
BM45.S235      2005                    200401090
296—dc22

Printed in the United States of America
1   3   5   7   9   10   8   6   4   2

This book is printed on acid-free paper. ∞

Book design by Marysarah Quinn

To Eve Rochelle Ilsen, dear friend, partner, spouse,

and

to my ordained students who continue the work of renewal

"We know not how we shall serve
the Lord our God until we get there."

—EXODUS 10:26

# CONTENTS

# INTRODUCTION

*S HWER TZU ZINE A YID*, our parents' generation used to say: it's hard to be a Jew. But we Jews living today are lucky. Being Jewish is safer now than at any time in history. Our challenge today is to be Jewish in a way that fills our lives with meaning. We want to be Jewish with *awareness*, to "do Jewish" in a way that satisfies our souls. We want our Yiddishkeit to enrich the world in which we live. In this book I make no assumptions about how much you know about Judaism, what holidays you keep, or whether you believe in God. I want us to put experience first, to start from your soul's experience and carry on from there.

A spiritual seeker is a person whose soul is awake, whose spirit has experienced—whether the mind knows it or not—that slap that gets the first breath going in a newborn. Such a soul is not content to stay on the level of mere observance,

ritual, and dogmatic belief that it encounters in most Jewish settings. It needs a more personal and mystical approach. It wants
an open-sky Judaism: a Judaism that invites the infinite and operates at a higher level of spiritual consciousness. It senses the divine
just beyond the surface of everyday existence and wants to connect to that. It yearns to achieve for itself those inner experiences that lie at the heart of religion's external forms. A mystical
approach to Judaism is therefore less dogmatic and more exper-
imental. It doesn't have a low ceiling, capping the mind and
frustrating its desire to unite in love and awe with a vital, living
universe. It is open-minded, open-souled. It says, "Try this. If
you feel it as a living reality, we're getting somewhere."

A mystical approach also recognizes that no static philosophy,
no one-size-fits-all Judaism, can express the entire range of our
inner growth. As we progress and develop, our spiritual needs will
change. I grew up with Judaism in my mother's milk, but before
committing myself intellectually to the Jewish path, I had to shed
the religion that I learned in the *cheders,* which spoke to me in
almost superstitious ways. In my teenage years the "old man in
the sky" was like a straitjacket. I couldn't think, or feel, or know
anything about that kind of God. I grew to adolescence during
the Holocaust. I witnessed the persecution and humiliation of our
people, including my own family. By the summer of 1939, when
I was fifteen years old, we had to flee our home in Vienna, where
I grew up, and cross the border illegally into Belgium, where we
lived a precarious existence. I was so angry with God, with Yiddishkeit, with everything I'd been taught. Where were all the rewards God had promised us? These, my *cheder* teachers said, were
reserved for *olam ha-ba,* the world to come. In *olam ha-ba* there

would be rivers of wine, and clothes would grow on trees, and the *Mashiach* would come; we'd be on top and the *goyim* on the bottom, and all the graves would open up and the dead would live again. I couldn't swallow these notions. My higher mind's immune system rejected them.

One weekend in Antwerp I said to myself, this Shabbos I'm going to get even with all that big rock-candy mountain nonsense. That afternoon I went to the local Orthodox youth study group, the same sort of group I used to attend in Vienna. I knew they were learning "Ethics of the Fathers," and sure enough a student began to read the introduction: "Every Jew has a portion of the world to come." "Pie in the sky!" I shouted. "Did anybody ever come back from there? It's all *narishkeit,* all rubbish. The opiate of the masses." I poured it all out—standing by the door for a quick getaway. The other students wanted to tear me apart, but the man sitting at the head of the table said, "Let him talk." When I finally had nothing more to say, the teacher said, "Would you like to hear from someone who agrees with you?" He asked for someone to bring Tractate Sanhedrin of the Talmud, turned to Maimonides' commentary on the Mishnah in the back, and started to read aloud. People have no idea what *olam ha-ba* is all about, Maimonides says. A blind man doesn't understand color; a eunuch doesn't understand sex. How could people living in this material world understand the pure godliness and spirit of the next?

This was so freeing. The teacher showed me that debunking foolish ideas was kosher, that our tradition had some precedents for that. He later introduced me to a group of young men who worked in Antwerp's diamond cutting trade and who, like him, had become Lubavitcher Hasidim. They would sit around cutting diamonds on those special lathes and studying Torah, and I joined them for a time. They listened seriously to my adolescent questions and encouraged me to find answers that rang true for me. Not only did they initiate me into the study of Hasidic texts, meditation, and introspection; they also gave me Romain Roland, a French writer and exponent of Hinduism, and Johannes Anker Larsen, a mystical Danish novelist and playwright. Instead of being confused, I was *in*-fused. My soul always seems to have felt the need to hang in tension between polar opposites, and this tension my mystical mentors provided with generosity. So even in the midst of teenage hopelessness I began to get glimpses of the Presence to which I ultimately devoted my life.

From then on I hungered for firsthand spiritual experience and sought out people who did Judaism on that level. My family fled to France, and there, too, I studied with the Lubavitch, a training in contemplation and soul transformation. We finally made it to New York, where I joined the Hasidim who studied and prayed with Reb Yosef Yitzchak, the sixth Lubavitcher Rebbe. And yet my soul still hung in tension, as the Rebbe recognized. When, years later, he sent me and my friend Shlomo Carlebach to reach out to Jewish kids in the colleges, I found that knowing the internal worlds of both doubt and faith helped me to comprehend their struggles.

I once brought some young college students to see Reb Yosef Yitzchak's successor, Reb Menachem Mendel Schneerson, the last Lubavitcher Rebbe. The Rebbe spoke to them for a little while, then asked if they had any questions. One young man raised his hand. "What is a rebbe good for?" he asked. Far from being offended, the Rebbe said: "That is a very good question. Let me tell you. It is written: 'You shall be unto me a land of desire' [Malachi 3:12]. The Earth contains all kinds of treasures, but you have to know where to dig. If you do not, you will come up with nothing but rocks or mud. But if you ask the geologist of the soul where to dig, you might find silver, which is the love of God; gold, which is awe before God; or diamonds, which is faith. A rebbe can only show you where to dig. You must do the digging yourself."

This book is an invitation to dig, to roll up your sleeves and get your hands dirty. Direct spiritual experience repays every effort we make to acquire it. In these pages, you will find boxes I've called "windows," which I hope might shed some extra light on different aspects of Yiddishkeit. You'll also find "doorways" that can help you gain entrance to our tradition. Please try them, and alter them to make them your own. I need you to be my active partners. If, as you read here, your heart answers "Yes!" then mark the spot. Share it with a friend; say, "Look, this is my thing. This speaks to me." In this way you will really begin to hear and feel what it is you need to do.

Throughout my life I have revised and readjusted my beliefs. I grew slowly, through study and prayer and God-wrestling and standing in the presence of great souls. I did not experience one seismic and pivotal moment but a long series of epiphanies, which often seemed unrelated to one another. Like a Zen student, I needed meditative and contemplative training to make sense of these "Aha!" moments. Ultimately, just as I grew into the world of the Lubavitch, I moved beyond it. I wanted to learn from the spiritually experienced of other faiths: Sufi sheikhs, Buddhist monks, Christian contemplatives, American savants. I received something from all of them. Today, I once again find myself in suspension between two polar opposites. To modern Jews, I am one of the last Mohicans of pre-Holocaust Jewish mysticism. As such I'm concerned about the continuity of our tradition and lineage and making it come alive for my own children, who, with so many Jews today, are searching for the balance between the values that are specific to Judaism and those that are universal. On the other foot, I stand on concern for our future—the future not only of our people but of the planet as a whole—and for the survival of the human race on our way to a great and divinizing transformation.

In a world where such a universalist spirituality is possible, why be Jewish? So many of my values connect me to nature, to the planet, to compassion for all living beings, that my Judaism at moments feels like a confinement—unless I begin to see that my Jewish values are the very ones that produced my universal concern. Today, I feel more than ever that we Jews are integral and necessary to life in the larger body of nations on planet Earth, that we need to be the healthy vital organ of the whole Earth that we are meant to be. By being the best and most enlightened Jews we can, we place ourselves at the service of all other beings with whom we share the here and now. If you, too, have felt the need to respond to the crisis of all living things; if in your heart you have heard your soul's whisper; if what you read here makes sense to you, I hope to inspire you to find and join with others—like-minded, like-feeling, and like-souled—to socialize your commitment, to become proactive, to be a world healer with the tools of our sacred tradition.

PART ONE

# THE TORAH
# OF TODAY

## CHAPTER 1

# OY, WHAT A WORD!

W E ALL FEEL spiritually hungry at different times in our lives, and we feel that hunger in different ways. Sometimes it is an absence that we feel, an ache, a yearning for something beyond what we experience day to day. We need someone to talk to sometimes, an Other with whom we can share our innermost thoughts—not a spouse or a lover, a parent or a friend, not even a therapist, but someone who is closer to us than all of these. Someone with whom to share those existential questions that besiege us in dark moments: "Does my life have any real meaning? Does the way I behave or what happens to me really matter? Will the world be safe for my children?" Someone to rage at: "Why me? Why is my life such a mess? Why are my kids (or my partner, or my boss) doing this to me? Why can't I make ends meet? Why am I ill? Why must a life be cut short before its time?" Someone to thank for the blessings in our lives, the superabundance of them or the few that remain to us: if you've had serious surgery, as I have, even something as simple as going to the bathroom without pain can bring on a feeling of "Thank goodness, my body is working right today."

Sometimes it is a presence that beckons or calls to us, a presence that reveals itself to us in glimpses. The other day, as day turned into evening, I was sitting down by a lake where I live. It was summertime. The fish were jumping. A dog was swimming in the water. The geese and the next generation of goslings were making their way around. On the horizon the Rocky Mountains, washed in pink light, rose up to the sky. It was so beautiful to see. I could feel a presence twinkling at me. "See, I'm right here. I am all this."

Perhaps you witnessed the birth of a child, or saw the new buds on the trees in spring, and felt the miracle of new life emerging in the world. Or maybe you stood at the deathbed of a loved one and thought you glimpsed their soul departing this world, leaving only their earthly shell behind. Sometimes it's a serendipity we experience, a crumb that life drops in our laps, a question answered *just like that,* a request granted out of the blue in a way that *couldn't* be just a coincidence—could it? Sometimes it's more extreme than that: a born-again mountaintop experience, a near-death or out-of-body experience, an epileptic aura, a vision of unity. Other times it feels like a warning from the universe, a stop sign that says to us, "You can't continue the way you've been going. You need to change your life before it's too late."

If you've ever felt the presence of—or yearning for—such a dimension to the world, you may have wondered: what is this feeling? What is it that I am experiencing? How can I connect to that more? How can I bring more beauty and connection and clarity into my daily life? And you may have wondered, too: Isn't such clarity and connection what religion is supposed to be about? Then why do I feel it so rarely in so-called "religious" settings?

These questions are at the heart of the spiritual searches of so many in our time, and they are beautiful questions. For such wondrous or painful experiences *are* the very stuff of religion. They were the seeds from which all religions grew, the nutrients that sustained and renewed them over time. They are still what religion *should* be about. The problem is that our ancient faiths have become ververbalized and underexperienced. We talk too much and feel too little. This is true of all world religions, but this book will be about Judaism, the faith in which I was raised and whose core teachings I have been striving all my life to understand and bring more fully alive. This book will not be about the Judaism of shalts and shalt nots, belief or theology, or even the Judaism of ethics, but about the Judaism of spiritual experience. Spiritual experience will be our departing point and our goal, and our constant companion along the way. How can Judaism— both old and new—help us lead more spiritual lives? How can Judaism help us search out spirituality, open the door to it, befriend it, and intensify it?

LET'S START WITH a question that is either a simple formality or the most difficult question of all. What shall we call this presence that we have felt? People the world over, in every culture and circumstance, have felt these things, this power, since time immemorial, and have given it many names. We in the Jewish tradition—and in many other traditions besides—have called it God.

GOD! Oy, what a word. Which handful of letters in the history of the world has accumulated more baggage than these? Martin Buber, in his book *Eclipse of God,* tells the story of a philosopher, Buber's host in a university town to which he had been invited, who protested passionately at Buber's use of the word. "How can you bring yourself to say 'God'?" the old man demands. "What word of human speech is so misused, so defiled, so desecrated as this?"

On the one hand, as the old saying goes, "Man's extremity is God's opportunity." When tragedy strikes, or great joy befalls us, or even when we're at the peak of sexual ecstasy—whenever an experience has shattered the usual language we use to describe such things—we have dialed that hotline to the center of the universe and said, in innumerable languages: "God! Oh, God!"

Too often, though, as soon as we catch ourselves at it, we hang up, quick. "Did you say 'God'?" Our internal prosecuting attorney jumps up with a list of objections as long as your arm. "That angry old man in the sky, that far-off 'other' who commands and keeps score and rewards and punishes? That God who stands by while innocents suffer, while children die of hunger every day? The God that the rabbis were always invoking: God commands this, God forbade that?" Most of us are still angry with the patriarchal, punitive God of our Hebrew schools and synagogues, prayer books and Bibles. We have so little stomach for this God business that we are barred from everything it brings in its wake.

Our internal prosecutor presses his case. "How do we even

know this God exists? What shred of evidence do we have that this God is anything more than a projection of human thought, an illusion woven together from all the prayers, the *Shema Yisraels* (Hear O Israels) that our people have murmured and shouted and sung and recited over the centuries? How can I take this God seriously? How can I take seriously anything this 'God' is supposed to have 'said'? What meaning does prayer have—prayer to what? to whom?"

These are all great questions, and Jews have been wrestling with them for centuries. Theologians have devoted their lives to constructing answers and systems we can live with.

But this is not a theological discussion. Theology is the after-thought of spiritual experience, not the other way around. We are not trying to construct some top-down authoritative system, but to nourish the seeds of our own personal spiritual experi-ence. We st

even rage,

fulness tow

questions li

of "God."

Has the

away, and al

and many r

term like G

experience

of trouble a

ness and my

the argumei

and acknowl

way of our experience." Judaism has a lot of very valuable spiritual tools built around the "God" concept. Later we will explore how each of us might give this God a more personal name,
a name that means more to us personally. For now, finding a way
to live with a thought named "God," to make it meaningful to
us—not by signing any belief statements, but by trying to imagine the entity that could be our partner in our "something out
there" experiences—will give us much better access to those
tools. We can then begin to explore them to see which might be
helpful to us in our search for deeper and more meaningful lives.

The Tibetan Buddhist lama Chögyam Trungpa, founder of
Naropa University in Boulder, where I teach, told a group of us
one day that his son had asked him, "Daddy, is there a God?"

"No," Trungpa told him.

"Phew," the little boy sighed. "I was scared there for a while!"

Trungpa was looking over at me, trying to bait me a little—
he was known for provocative behavior. So I looked back at him
and said, "The god that you don't believe in, I don't believe in,
ither."

e all have images of God that the past has bequeathed to us,
times these images get in the way. But these images are
ey are just images of God. "God language" can be
us in relating to the infinite, but we should not
real thing. If we are to have some hope of re-
inspired our ancestors to invent the word,
ibility of having "God" be our vehicle
meaning, we need to clean the
to scrape off a few of the bar-
ree common objections to

the concept and suggest ways we might soften those objections—
not refute them decisively, by any means, but find ways to live
with them, ways of framing the concept of "God" that will allow us to say, "Okay, we accept this for now. We can drop the
mental quotation marks around 'God.' Let's continue our search
for spiritual experience."

*"If there is a god, then that god is me, all of us, animals, trees, rocks,
everyday—not some personified Other who 'wants' our prayers or our
obedience."*

Maybe so, though an infinite God could *include* such an Otherness as well. But the point, in our nontheological, experience-
based approach, is not what God "wants" or doesn't want; God,
however we understand the concept, can take care of Godself.
The point is what *we* want and need. In those moments when
we feel the need to send out appreciation, or thanks, or pleading,
or sorrow, or rage—not to a specific human target but to the
universe—we send it out to an Other. To that philosopher in our
head—or among our friends, or our family—we can say, "This
is the God that I need right now. Cut me some slack. You can
come back with your objections later."

Our ego or intellect, our reasoning, analytical, critical function, is perhaps our most sophisticated survival mechanism and
a wonderfully life-enhancing tool besides. But it is generally no
friend to spiritual experience. Spiritual counselors have pointed
out that much of their counseling to those who are spiritually
troubled deals with the ego's resistance to one's inner spirit and

to God. All world religions spent a good deal of time and genius developing ways to circumvent this quick and ever-watchful faculty. As the mystical work known as the *Tikkunei Zohar* says, "Not by thought can we grasp you, but only through the desire of the heart."

Sooner or later we realize that the intellect, powerful as it is, will never be up to the job. The intellect will only be satisfied with an utterly abstract god, a god that is All, that is infinite in time and space. Now, infinity and eternity are wonderful mind stretchers, but they don't always speak to the heart. How long does it take our sun to go around our galaxy? About 230 million years for a single trip. Such figures quickly begin to lose significance. Millions of years? Nanoseconds? Life on the timescale of a galaxy or a gluon would be meaningless to us. We're looking for a partner to our innermost feelings. We need finitude at times. If we took three quintillion steps toward an infinite God, we would still be an infinite distance apart.

My concern is with human experience and human scale. From an astrophysical perspective, there's no difference between chocolate and dog poop. On an atomic or subatomic scale there's no difference either. From the point of view of my experience and needs, however, there's a big difference. Philosophy and abstraction are all very well, but I just want to make sure that we keep the human perspective. On the human level we answer the philosophical objections with humility, saying, "This is where I want to go right now. That's all I can talk about for the moment." My heart needs a dualistic relationship, a "me" and a "you," an "I-Thou" relationship, in Buber's words. Every so often, for fleeting moments here and there, the spiritually advanced among us might dissolve in the infinite. But as soon as we're done dissolving, we're back to the feeling of "I yearn for you," or "I want to dissolve in that again." Such longing and yearning for an Other is itself a very precious part of our spiritual lives.

*"Fine, we're bringing it down to the level of human experience—but what about all the human language that's used to describe God? I can't connect to language like 'O Father, O King.' All this anthropomorphic, authoritarian, sexist language gets in my way."*

This very fruitful objection assumes three things, all of which are true. First, that our experience of the infinite, the numinous, is inseparable from the language we use to describe it: our choice of language will inevitably color our relationship to the infinite at that moment. Second, that our "God language" is not a divine, God-given absolute: the metaphors that we use for the divine are rooted in and shaped by our particular human history and culture. And third, that our linguistic interface to God must evolve as our culture and spiritual needs evolve.

We start, again, from experience. Anyone who has had a truly "spiritual" moment, a moment of breaking through our day-to-day reality and touching the divine, knows how difficult it is to communicate that experience to others—or even to recapture it later for ourselves. The mind doesn't have the wherewithal to wrap around what the soul knows. So in come Kabbalah and Hasidism and Vedanta and Vajrayana Buddhism and Christian mysticism, each system trying to give us the language to handle such experiences, each with its own vocabulary. Indeed, religions

might be seen as elaborate, multilayered metaphors, with layers
upon layers of submetaphors, constructions that point beyond
themselves toward the primary experience of ultimate reality
but do not capture it.

Anyone who has a spiritual breakthrough will reach for the
language of his or her culture and spiritual system to describe it.
So imagine a Hindu on a mountaintop who after days of fasting
and meditation suddenly sees through the whole world. How is
he going to talk about it afterward, even to himself? The only
thing he can remember is "Shivo-hum," I am Shiva. "I was Shiva,
I tell you, I was there, I had a glimpse of the moment in which
Shiva utterly destroys everything, I experienced that annihilation, I *was* that moment, don't ask me how it went, but it was
the most precious experience I've ever had in my life, and whatever I can do to convince other people of this reality will be a
real mitzvah."

If a skeptic had just then popped out of the crowd and said,
"Just a minute. How could you, a man of flesh and blood, possibly know what it's like to be Shiva?" the holy man might have
said, "Nu, so I wasn't Shiva" and quietly gone on his way. If the
holy man had a following, though, a disciple would have quickly
written down, "The master said 'I am Shiva,'" and after that
would have come generations of interpretation and argument so
as not to deviate from the secretary's version of the holy man's
primary experience.

This is the kind of language we have inherited today. Each
religion's language was shaped and colored by the history and
worldly experience of its adherents. The peoples of the ancient
Near East, where Judaism began, were ruled by local kings—

chieftains, really—and the regional superpower, the king of kings. Today the word *king* brings to mind an antiquated and tyrannical form of government that our modern democracies have rightfully replaced. In those days, however, the king of kings was the closest thing one could imagine to a god. He was a remote, all-powerful, barely imaginable figure who meted out life and death at will, whose favor could be bounteous but whose punishment, when provoked, was swift and terrible.

The god that Abraham imagined was closer to a "superduper king" of his time than to the abstraction of later philosophers. How does a local chieftain relate to such a king? He makes a covenant, a *b'rit* (or bris), with him. When a local king wanted the protection of Suppiluliumas, great king of the Hittites, for example, he came to Suppiluliumas and asked to make a covenant. "I will pay you such and such a tribute every year and send one of my children to be in your court. You will protect me from my enemies. And we call heaven and earth and the sun and moon and all the stars and all your gods and all my gods to witness this covenant." When you become convinced that there is a force out there that overrides even a king like Suppiluliumas, and you want to ally yourself with that power, you make a covenant with the *melekh malkhei ha-m'lakhim,* as our *Alenu* prayer says— the "king of king of kings." And since the earthly kings all had their soldiers and ministers and satraps, each with a different rank and title, pretty soon a member of your household asks, "Does God have soldiers like that?"

"What do you mean? Of course! *Adonai tzeva'ot shemo,* He is the Lord of Hosts!" And you begin to imagine all the angels and cherubim and seraphim standing around, singing God's praises and doing his work for him. Ideas need to be pictured. Why else would the ancients have made sculptures of wood or stone and abased themselves in front of them? Why else would they want to worship and appease that piece of wood if it weren't for the need to celebrate infinity in the most finite and focused way?

Modern Judaism, on the other hand, has gone to the opposite extreme. Idol smashing—iconoclasm—is a cornerstone of our faith, but in our zeal to fulfill the Torah's prohibition against graven images we have reduced God to a concept. What can we say about this God? Well, God is omniscient, omnipotent, omnipresent. That's fine, but it doesn't give me a God I can relate to. It doesn't give me a language to express the desire to connect that wells up inside me sometimes.

Both extremes went wide of the mark. Our notion of God, so revolutionary in the region at the time, could not possibly be comprehended through statues of stone. But to those who yearn for spiritual experience, a formless, abstract idea is not enough, either. Yes, God is galaxies and gluons and the great void beyond, but then we have no one to talk to.

If you say, "You're anthropomorphizing the infinite by personalizing it," I readily admit it. But what is it that I want? I want a connection. I want spiritual intimacy. We are hungry for cosmic companionship. We want someone or something to talk to who is not our parents or partner or children or therapist or friends—who is all of these, but more. Our soul needs this. "But it's all one big mental construct," the intellect says, and I agree. But I begin not with my mind but with my imagination, and imagining a God I can talk to gives me satisfaction on a very basic level. Take a look: life has satisfaction circuits built in. Na-

ture itself has built in positive feedback loops that reinforce behavior. Food tastes good. Giving birth is a daunting task, so we
have a heavy satisfaction circuit—the joys of sex—built in. On a
higher level, there is a satisfaction circuit built in when I call
upon the spirit of the universe, a circut that tells me, "This is
good for you. Keep doing it."

And so, through the ages, we have reached for names, for
metaphors. From our earliest ancestors to our Bubbeh or Zaida
calling out *"Gottenyu!"* we knew that we needed an interface
between the finite and the infinite. We could not thank, cry to,
or call on an abstraction: we had to put a face on it, to give the
object of our outpourings a name. No name can capture the infinite, but each name lends us a way of focusing *toward* the infinite,
of achieving a feeling of relatedness. The ancients called upon
their gods by name—El, Hathor, Baal, Zeus—as we address one
another by name today. The name stood for the named, a one-
to-one equivalence. As our conception of the divine became
deeper and more multifaceted, we realized that all these names
were but aspects of the One. We began to develop what Hebrew
calls *kinnuyim:* not proper, given names but appellations, descriptions, or characterizations that gradually gained currency
through the centuries.

Judaism has had many of these, and each took on its own
particular flavor. So *Adonai* or "Lord" means the one who calls the
shots. With the Lord as my shepherd, what can I lack? *Elohim*
has traditionally emphasized the attribute of divine justice. *Yah* of
all names is the most onomatopoeic, evoking the breath of life
itself. *Shekhinah* welcomes the female presence of God, who
abides among us when we are connected and pines in exile

when we are cut off from our roots and from the ground of our being. *Ha-Makom,* the Place, connotes a presence or holy space wherein *we* abide. When on the high holidays we sing *Avinu malkeinu,* "Our Father, Our King," we mean that greater than any parent is the parent of all creation, whose ways we aspire to accept absolutely. When we chant *El rachum ve-chanun,* "merciful and grace-giving God," we mean the healer of karma, the one who helps us with the wrongs we have done.

We have names of awesome and unfathomable mystery, like the untranslatable *Shaddai,* and shape-shifting names, like the name with which God introduced himself to Moses: *Ehyeh asher ehyeh,* "I will be what I will be." And of course we have YHVH, the tetragrammaton, the name even the High Priest himself would utter only once a year as he prayed for the people on Yom Kippur in the Holy of Holies. To pronounce such a name regularly would be to rob it of its power, so we started building fences around it. During prayer or Torah reading we pronounce those letters "Adonai," but outside of these prescribed circumstances we avoid even that, using "ha-Shem," the Name, instead. In Jewish legends, the Holy Name could split mountains and dispel demons. To Kabbalists, each letter represents another dimension of reality—four worlds, four levels of soul, four forces in the universe, four parts of the human body created in the image of God. To them, though, even the tetragrammaton came with a set of associations. When they wanted to refer to the One before creation, before any *thought* of creation, they said *En-Sof:* endless, infinity. Why *"En-Sof,"* endless, and not *"En-Techilah,"* beginning-less? Because they wanted to emphasize God's reality.

*En-Sof* extends outward in every dimension. It encompasses not only the *what* of God but the *where, when, why,* and *how* as well.

Not all of these names are so solemn and formal. Yiddish is especially rich in nicknames for God, epithets that combine love and awe and not a little humor. *Gottenyu,* little God, is the homey God, the one you can always come to with your kvetching. *Der Aybishter* means, literally, the most high. On the humorous level it means the guy upstairs, the one who shoves furniture around in the middle of the night—you're never quite sure why, but you're resigned to it. But the Lubavitcher Rebbe would begin many of his blessings with *"Der Aybishter zol helfen,"* may the Most High help such-and-such to happen, and we always had a sense, *"Der Aybishter farginnt,"* the Highest One won't begrudge us, he wants us to have these things. Yiddish had many such appellations. "Oy, *heiliger basheffer,* holy creator, grant peace to your struggling creations." The name I myself use most often is Hebrew, but I pronounce it in the Galician Yiddish rendition of my childhood: *Ribboyno shel oylom,* Master of the Universe. This is the God that listens to me when I need to reach out, the God I am intimate with.

These names are like "heart accounts" that our people have invested in through the ages. Every time someone cried out a name of God, they made a deposit to that account. These accounts have been there for centuries now, collecting interest. They are part of our ancestors' legacy to us, available for anyone to access; all we need to do is make a withdrawal with understanding and sincerity. These names, these heart accounts, are one of the paths our traditions offer us to make a connection, to achieve spiritual intimacy. Their currency has been greatly devalued in our time, but they still have the power to move us—if we let them. We should not be too quick to throw them away.

Yet just as our interfaces with the infinite evolved over time, so must we continue to slowly open new accounts, to evolve names for the infinite that ring true for us today. We are quick to resent images of God that don't fit. They infantilize and disappoint us. But why do we react this way? Could it be because they fall short of the images of God that we long for? I believe that even some of the most hardened and skeptical among us have felt, in their heart of hearts, "If only God could mean this to me." This is exemplified most touchingly in the movie *Dead Man Walking,* when Sister Prejean promises a convicted rapist and murderer that she will be "the face of God" for him in the final moments before his execution, a visage of the divine mercy and forgiveness that he cannot find in the human society that will, the following day at dawn, strap him to a gurney and pump a fatal dose of earthly justice into his veins. This is the great power of our names and metaphors for God. They are our gateways to the infinite. If we call upon them, no matter what our extremity, they will open the way for us.

## DOORWAY:
## FINDING YOUR OWN NAME FOR GOD

What is the face of God that you long for in your deepest moments? Is it a friend you need? Or a comforter? A rock you can lean on when you are most besieged? A recipient of your joy and thanks? An address for your prayers for yourself or your loved ones?

Can you give that face of God a name? Try it. See what wells up inside you. Take a quiet moment, or wait until some joy or sorrow opens your heart. Perhaps it will be a name from our tradition, perhaps something you make up. Whenever you feel the need to reach out, say that name. Repeat it over and over to yourself. Say it out loud if you can. Try it out on your tongue. Savor it. Open an account for yourself. Start making a connection.

## DEEPENING OUR VOCABULARY

Those who protest the limitations language imposes on our grasp of the infinite make a valuable point. I believe that evolving names and ways of speaking to God that work for each individual and community is an important part of making a spiritual connection. Using such language out of a sense of understanding and choice, rather than having it imposed upon us, does a great deal to counter the infantilizing effect that gets us to raise such objections in the first place. In trying to expand and deepen our understanding of God as much as possible, we must also refine our understanding of the blinders that our terminology— and even the very structure of our language—often imposes.

One problem with the word *god* is that *god* is a noun. Almost all of our names and appellations for God are nouns. You remember the simple definition of a noun as it was first given to us in grade school: a noun is the name of a person, place, or thing. By defining "God" exclusively as a noun we "thingify" or objectify God in our minds, no matter how often we protest that God is free from all the properties of matter, beyond time and space, and so on. How can we begin to conceive of an Infinite Being, an Absolute All that is in no way a thing? We must expand beyond the language of nouns, of objects.

I have for many years encouraged my students to think of God as a verb. Imagining God in terms of action, of process, opens up new ways of connecting to the infinite. Take the expression "Infinite Being" in the previous paragraph. If we think of God as a process of Be-ing, of is-ing, of infinite existing, we open up new ways of relating. We can begin to imagine a "godding," a process that the universe is doing, has been doing, and will continue to do—at least on our scale of comprehension—forever. In the largest sense, we can say that as part of that universe we are "godding" in everything we do. In the more limited, human sense, we could wake up in the morning and consider how we might "god" most effectively today.

Different ways of thinking and talking about God are appropriate to different needs and levels of understanding. If my children asked me, "Abba, is there a God?" I would say, "Yes, there is a God." But if you ask me for a categorical statement: "Does God exist?" I might demur, because "is-ing" and "existing" aren't the same thing. Existing has a more limited sense: a table exists, a mountain exists. Their existence is finite, at least in our limited, everyday understanding. Their existence begins here and ends there. But when the first commandment says, "I am the

Lord thy God," I get a sense, through thinking of God as a verb, that God's "I AM-ing" is infinitely deeper than any concept I could possibly have of my own.

Too abstract? Perhaps. The important point here is to open up new vistas of god-thought and to realize that even the objections to "god-language" fall into the limitations they would have us transcend. To those who say, "God is none of these attributes and appellations," I would say, "Right. But go further. Think of God not as the subject of your sentence, who is or is not this or that, but as the *is*-ing, the very process of being itself."

Thinking of God as a verb has its limitations, too, of course. English verbs have two forms. Transitive verbs have direct objects: *She gave me a book.* Intransitive verbs do not require a direct object: *She gave generously.* They can be active or passive: We *love* and *are loved.* I have for years encouraged my students to imagine the God verb as *interactive,* a form that barely exists in English. Imagine a flag waving in the wind, said Buddhist monk Thich Nhat Hanh. Without the wind, the flag would not wave. Without the flag, the wind could not do the waving. Flag and wind are inseparable at that moment: they are interwaving. In this perception we have no subject or object, no active or passive, no "each" and no "other," but rather a single and indivisible phenomenon. So it is with God and creation, the world and the process that underlies it, that *is* it. We get a more Zen-like, instantaneous-flash-of-total-recognition grasp of the whole picture this way.

God in our expanded understanding can be all parts of speech. We don't use the adjective "godly" much anymore, as in "She was a godly woman" or "That was a godly deed," but we should bring it back. How might we be more godly men and women? How might we make a given act more godly? How might we raise the godliness of any given situation that we find ourselves in?

*"You talk as if 'God' were synonymous with 'good.' How can a people that lived through the Holocaust still harbor any illusions about the goodness of God? What about all the evil in the world? How can I even have the chutzpah to thank God for my own blessings when I know that my neighbor—as good a person as I am—is dying from cancer, or that children are starving in the world?"*

"If God is God, He is not good," wrote poet Archibald MacLeish in *JB,* his play in verse based on Job. "If God is good, He is not God." This weighty problem comes up in every serious discussion about the existence of God. Theodicy, the philosophers call it: the problem of God's justice. The world is so full of evil on every scale, from genocide to a single innocent child abused. How can we subscribe to a God that allows this? How can we talk of God's justice, far less God's mercy? On the other hand, how can we take seriously any idea of a God that doesn't encompass evil as well as good?

To this question, again, we have no airtight theological answer. We can only offer a few ways of thinking about the problem that might help to allow and perhaps deepen our subjective experience.

WE ARE ATTACHED to the idea of a good God, just as we are attached to the idea of a good parent. We want God to love us, to cherish us, to protect us from harm. We can see how we might deserve some unpleasantness for our transgressions, if that's the way the universe really works, but those punishments should be fair. A God who abandons us is a deadbeat God, unworthy of our allegiance.

These attachments and expectations quickly shatter in the face of reality. We see the innocent suffering all the time. It is startling how often the expression "only the good die young" comes to pass, how often the best and most inspiring among us get stricken with cancer or die in an accident. WHY? we feel like shouting. "Why does that wonderful, gentle, righteous person have to die?" or "Why me?" or "Why my child?" Sooner or later some of us may feel, "If it's for this you created me, God, you could have saved yourself the trouble." Can you imagine how those who lived during the Holocaust may have said, as Job did, "Cursed is the day my mother conceived me"?

We cannot possibly express genuine love of God or our fellow beings if we always put a lid on this kind of existential anger. If we do not express this anger, we turn it on ourselves. Just as you might send out thanks to the universe when you feel lucky or blessed, take the time to send out your rage as well. No one who hasn't taken a vigil for the night and had it out with God can get to the place where their love and faith become real. We see a magnificent example of such rage in the movie *The Apostle*. Sonny, a Southern preacher, a deeply religious, enormously charismatic, and yet tragically flawed man, suddenly has his family life shattered and his beloved church taken away from him. His life in pieces around his feet, Sonny retreats to the house he grew up in, where he paces back and forth in his undershirt until dawn, sweating and shaking his fists, raging and shouting and pleading with his God. "I can't take it! Give me a sign or something. Blow this pain out of me. Give it to me tonight, Lord God Jehovah. If you won't give me back my wife, give me peace. I don't know who's been foolin' with me, you or the Devil. . . . But I'm confused, I'm mad—I love you, Lord, I love you, but *I am mad at you*. So deliver me tonight. What should I do? Should I lay hands on myself? What should I do? I'm your servant. I always called you Jesus, you've always called me Sonny. What should I do, Jesus?"

The Hasidic master Rabbi Nachman of Bratslav, no stranger to depression and disappointment, illness and untimely death, offered a startling response to living with the problem of evil. He points to the liturgy of *Ne'ilah,* the final prayer of Yom Kippur, in which the pleading congregation invokes Abraham, Isaac, and Jacob in turn. "Abraham knew you from youth," we begin. The usual interpretation, of course, is that Abraham, the progenitor of monotheism, embraced the idea of God when he was still a young man. But Rabbi Nachman reads the line as meaning, "Abraham knew you from *your* youth," as if to say, "We knew you from the beginning of human relationship with you, when you were still young in the God business." Nachman seems to recognize that God, too, is still learning. We are struggling together.

Rabbi Nachman was not the only one to consider this idea. The whole Torah—from the Garden of Eden to the Flood to Abraham to Moses and beyond—can make much more sense if we think of God as an emergent God, evolving hand in hand with humanity and creation. Like many such pronouncements, Nachman's formulation would seem heretical if taken as absolute.

On the experiential level, though, it helps us to understand and accept the evil in the world by imagining an infinite that, at least as manifested in the human sphere, is learning and evolving along with us over time.

We, too, grow over the course of our lives, and suffering is one of our teachers. Only after suffering destroys Job's cozy, logical view of God does he arrive at the point where he says, "Even though he slay me, yet I trust in him." We prefer that a child not learn this lesson right away. We want to give as much security as we can. Time enough to challenge their sense of safety! To a child we say, "God is good. I thank God for my food. Now I lay me down to sleep and ask the Lord my soul to keep, and if I die before I wake I ask the Lord my soul to take." To a childish understanding, whether in an individual or a people, we start by saying, "God will reward you if you do good, and punish you if you err." Verse after verse in sacred texts the world over testify on that level. But as we move through the moral dilemmas of our lives, as we gradually ascend to higher levels of moral development, we may come to a place like the people in the gas chambers screaming out *Shema Yisrael:* I know my Redeemer liveth, yet I know that I have to die in this world, that it won't help. Such affirmation in the very jaws of death can only come from a higher understanding.

The question of theodicy can stop our spiritual conversation cold if we let it, but we should not. It's a useful question, like a bone a dog chews on from time to time in order to sharpen his teeth. It challenges our complacency. How much of the evil in the world are we responsible for? Is that cancer, that road death, that famine purely arbitrary, or did we contribute to it in some far-removed way? Without absolving God or the perpetrators, did we bear any responsibility at all for an event like September 11, or even (heresy of heresies) the Holocaust? Theodicy can throw us back on ourselves that way.

Theodicy teaches us, too, to avoid loading our concept of God with a positive charge in too simplistic a way. Swami Satchidananda, the yogic master, has a good way of saying it: "Don't make any appointments, you won't have dis-appointments." We make a certain appointment with the word *god*. God loves good and hates evil, God wants this and doesn't want that, God would not allow for such and such a thing to happen. We make God the steward of morality and build up expectations, expectations that sooner or later are bound to be shattered. If instead we strive to accept all sides of the equation, if we could get into a Möbius strip mentality in which both sides of the page, good and evil, are one and the same, then we start to get a real sense of that famous phrase from *Adon Olam: "Ve-hu echad ve-ein sheini,"* God is one, there is no other.

A POET by the name of David Slabotsky, who wrote wonderful little vignettes, tells the following story. Rabbi Ishmael was teaching his disciples all about the names of God, how this name meant this, and that power of God is invoked with that name. And then he said, "But God is *none* of those names."

One of his disciples protested. "But Rabbi, that's a contradiction."

Rabbi Ishmael thought for a moment and said, "Yes. But only a contradiction."

Contradictions we can live with. Nothing we can say about God will survive the rigors of logical analysis. But that shouldn't get in the way of our search for the presence we have felt in our most spiritually open—or spiritually hungry—moments. If there is a tension between what we know in our minds and what we feel in our hearts, then let's stay with that tension. If there is a contradiction, let us take it upon ourselves. Only let us press on with our desire to experience the numinous and serve the patterns of the universe in a deeper, more meaningful way.

## WINDOW: UNDERSTANDING FAITH

Judaism places far less emphasis on faith than do other religions. We have always been a religion of deeds. Perform the mitzvot, the commandments, classical Judaism teaches, and faith will take care of itself. Most of us today don't operate that way. We need to feel an urge, an inner whispering that says, "Follow, I will take you. If you want to be more awakened, follow this." That inner whispering is the beginning of faith.

Weighing the notion of faith as we would any other logical proposition can make us uneasy. Better is to simply try to imagine it. What might faith feel like?

Faith is what I call a mind-move, a radical shift in awareness. The expression "a leap of faith" is so true. Faith is not something we can arrive at by a careful, step-by-step process. It is not something we can square with our intellect. Faith does not make sense, nor does it feel safe. It is what takes us further after the questions that can be answered logically have been exhausted. To have faith, we must let go. Faith is like swimming the backstroke, reaching above and behind us into an unknown we cannot see. Faith is like driving forward with only the rearview mirror as a guide. Some might even reason their way to the place where there is a God. But the *quality,* the *essence,* the *whatness* of God—that we can only reach with the opening-up, the joyful surrender, that is faith. To experience faith even for a moment we must make a leap beyond intellect, beyond logic. A leap into the beyond.

A story is told of the Indian saint Ramakrishna, who stands in front of an image of the Hindu goddess Kali. "I have served you," he tells her, "and you have not answered me. I love you, I sing to you, I worship you, I adore you—and you have not manifested yourself to me. A life in which you don't bother to answer me is not worth living." And with that he grabs Kali's ritual dagger and is about to throw himself upon it, when at the very last moment the presence of Kali engulfs him.

The point of this story, to me, is not some miraculous event. It is that only when Ramakrishna, after all that pleading and singing and worship and adoration, finally breaks through the last mental barrier and is ready to offer his very life—only then does Kali become real to him.

Even the great Jewish teachers have been mystified by the problem of faith. Once Reb Schneur Zalman of Liadi, founder of the Lubavitch movement, was musing aloud to one of his followers.

"Moshe," he says to him. "Nu, tell me, what is God? What is soul, Moshe? What is faith?"

"Rebbe," the disciple says, "you're the master. *I* should tell *you?*"

"But what do you think, Moshe?" the Rebbe persists.

"I don't know!"

The Rebbe sighed. "I don't know either. But maintain we must, and affirm we must, that that which clearly exists and besides which nothing else clearly exists—that is God."

The Rebbe stroked his beard for a few minutes and thought some more. "And what is soul, Moshe? Soul is that being that knows with certainty that God exists and that besides God nothing else clearly exists.

"And faith, Moshe? Faith is the *way* the soul knows that God exists and that besides God nothing clearly exists."

In our day we lack even this degree of certainty. We replace the Rebbe's "must" with questions. Can we, if only for fleeting moments, affirm an Ultimate Existence? Can we get in touch with that part of us that truly knows that dimension of existence?

This story also teaches us that God is not some independent "out there" entity. God, soul, and faith—the known, the knower, and the knowing—are inseparable. We are one.

## DEEPENING OUR UNDERSTANDING

If we can move away from worrying about absolute and yet somehow static questions like "Does God exist"; if we can accept that one way, at least, into deeper spiritual experience lies in stepping away from total abstraction and toward more concrete images and action; if we can use a certain amount of personified "God talk" in our search to deepen our relationship to this presence we feel in the universe—then we start to enter a whole different universe of discourse. We can begin to explore questions like, "What do I do with this yearning? How do I progress?" We can start asking ourselves: What is incubating inside of me? What am I pregnant with? Something is stirring in me. I feel contractions. I can't continue with the status quo. On the other hand, how many times have I felt birth pangs—intentions, the beginnings of conviction—but nothing lasting has come of it, nothing has survived that neonatal stage, nothing has really changed in my life. How can I learn to nurture and sustain the spirituality that is a-borning inside me?

We need to enter into a dialogue with that presence we have felt.

I believe that we are all theotropic beings. Just as a sunflower turns toward the sun and we call it *helio*tropic, I believe that all beings are *theo*tropic: we grow naturally toward God. In Saul Bellow's novel *Henderson the Rain King* there's a guy with a voice that keeps saying, "I want, I want." Every so often he asks, "What do you want?" But the voice just keeps on saying, "I want, I want." There is something about being alive that says to us, "I want." No matter what we give it, it isn't satisfied, because that "I want" wants nothing less than infinity: it wants it all.

What I mean here is not some grasping need for material or emotional gratification, but the stirrings of an entity that I could call soul, *neshamah* in Hebrew. Years ago when my daughter was young she once asked me, "Abba, when you're asleep, you can wake up, right?"

"Right," I answered.

"So when you're awake," she said, "can you wake up even more?"

That part of us that always seeks to awaken even more, I call soul. Judaism speaks of the soul as a spark of God. I like to think of the soul as a holographic snippet off the old block. Each spark, each snippet, contains the all.

There's a wonderful Jewish teaching about an angel that teaches us the entire Torah when we are in our mother's womb and then, just before we are born, taps us under the nose (which gives us that hollow above our lip), and we forget it all. This memory loss, to me, bespeaks that tendency, that pull that we all have toward a point of origin that we once knew but now must strive to recall. The image of forgetfulness in the story is crucial: forgetting something is not the same as never knowing it in the first place. Even those things that we seem to have forgotten completely are merely dormant, like a spore that has been planted within us, waiting for the proper conditions to germinate and grow.

This soul; this spore; this snippet off the holographic block; this teaching that each of us has learned and forgotten but that lurks deep in our memories—all of these images point to an intricate dance between the God that is us, each individual creation, and the God that is All. In the various dramas of our lives, we often forget the truth of our godliness and think of ourselves only as separate. In the early years of our development to adulthood and sometimes for long periods afterward, this feels perfectly okay. Being an individual is fun. It is what we all strive toward as we mature. It feels in some very deep way like the right way to be. But sooner or later, as we get older, perhaps have children, start to sense our own mortality, we begin to feel that pull toward the All. At first we try to ignore it. We hear "I want" and we go to the fridge. Our soul wants so bad that we feel physical pain, so we reach for a pill. We feel edgy and restless, so we plan a vacation, try to "get away." Years of distraction and estrangement later we are still feeling lonely in some profound way, and lost.

But we are not cut off. In rare and fleeting moments of grace we feel a shot of love pouring into us, the creations, from the creator. Hasidism teaches, furthermore, that the worldly delights with which we try so hard to assuage our spiritual hunger themselves contain a spark of holiness, for they echo the holy love we once knew before separation. The Baal Shem Tov (c. 1700–1760), founder of Hasidism, taught that our attraction to these delights is precisely what makes it possible for us to love God. If these worldly desires had not been etched into our bodies, we would never develop the sensitivity needed for spiritual being. Thus the obstacles to what the Hasidim call *devekut,* adhering to God, can serve as the very cement that adheres us to God.

This frees us to delight in our individuality, the unique stamp of creation that each of us bears and embodies. The spark of delight in being separate, to the Baal Shem, resides in the intention and goal of the separation, which is to put our individuality at the service of union, of Oneness. We whose hunger is unfulfilled feel the glimmerings of that intention, but have not yet found a way to carry it out.

So we dance, God the creator and God the created. We separate, come close, and separate again. The quest is, in a sense, about how we might more consciously join that dance—and how we as partners might start to lead rather than follow, to develop more sure-footed moves of our own.

This is no easy matter. It's all very well to say that our goal as spiritual beings is to put our selves at the service of union, but what does that really mean? How do we go about it? More pointedly, how do we go about it without losing our individuality and in the context of our daily lives?

The Jewish path toward answers, as we know, lies in asking more questions. Not just any questions, but the big questions, the ones that are nearest to our hearts. When we identify the questions that we want to throw out to the universe, to God, we will know the points where God really touches us, where we and our cosmic partner in this dance most closely and consciously embrace.

What knowledge are we hungry for? What values do we hold so high in our own lives that we would be prepared, if necessary, to pay dearly for them—even to die for them? From what sources do we draw those highest values? What do we care most about, and where do the wellsprings of our caring come from? What is the most basic story of our lives, the story that we ourselves are living, through days, months, years, generations? What is the most important story or stories that we want to pass on to our children?

Asking important questions is far more important than answering them, and of course no one can ask your questions for you, far less answer them. For the searching soul any answer sooner or later begins to get stale anyway. What I will try to do in this book is to suggest ways in which Judaism, our centuries-old and endlessly deep tradition, might help you wrestle with your questions—after all, we Jews have been wrestlers since our forefather Jacob took on the angel—and help you, too, to deepen your quest and fill it with joy. At the same time, I am only too painfully aware of how my tradition has *failed* to help people with their deepest questions and struggles. Part of my own story, my own struggle, has been to find ways to reframe and renew the tradition I was brought up with, that it might once again uplift and inspire us to live more fully in the world today.

# CHAPTER 2

# A LIFE IN TIME

*EEP! BEEP! BEEP! BEEP! BEEP!*
Is it really time to get up already? I'm so tired. I have to get to the shower. Then coffee. Ah, that's good. Okay, now, hurry, get the kids off to school. Look at the time! I have to leave for the office.

All right, here I am. Check e-mail. Oy, look at all those messages! Can't get to them now—time for the meeting. These meetings go on forever. I better get myself some coffee.

Noon: Thank goodness, time to go to the gym. Headphones on, music on, machine on. Run! CNN on the overhead screen says the markets are down again today. Back to work.

Finally, it's time to go home. Pick up the kids, go to the store— oh, and drop off those shirts at the dry cleaner's. Listen to messages. Then it's getting supper on the table and the kids through

their evening routine. With any luck I'll have time to watch a
little TV or read for a few minutes before I go to bed. . . .

## LIVING IN ORGANIC TIME

We spend most of our days living in "commodity time." Just as
our movements take us down a particular path over the course of
our day, so does our daily life occupy a certain segment along the
axis of time. In commodity time the points along that segment—
when we get up, eat, work, exercise, spend time with our loved
ones, go to sleep—are dictated not so much by our physical needs,
far less our emotional or spiritual ones, as by the demands of
running an efficient marketplace.

In commodity time we are our own worst taskmasters. "I need
a nap," my body says, and I say, "Later. Here, have some more coffee." "I'm hungry." "No time for a real meal now. Eat this burger
and fries, quick." "I have to go to the bathroom." "Soon, soon."
"I need to stretch my legs." "Later!" When I live like this I'm always denying something that a Zalman inside of me wants.

If I want to be a democracy rather than a dictatorship, those
other Zalmans have to have a chance, too. This is why whenever
someone asks me, "I want to get into Judaism more—what
should I do?" I say, "Do Shabbos first." I like to use the Yiddish
word *Shabbos* for Sabbath: it gives that same warm feeling to my
*kishkes,* my insides, as the day itself. Whatever term you favor, if
you want to get more Judaism into your life, start with some
form of Shabbos practice, maybe just twenty minutes or an hour

at first, but ultimately building toward taking a day of rest each week to reconnect to more natural rhythms.

Sabbaths are like periods inserted into an otherwise endless run-on sentence. They help us know when it is time to stop and take a breath. They remind us to take a weekly break from living in commodity time to reanchor ourselves in what we might call "organic time," a way of living more in tune with our own deepest needs—as well as those of our family and the entire community and society of which we are a part.

The innovations of modern society, wonderful as they are, cut us off from organic time. Night falls and we override it with the flick of a switch. Winter sets in: we turn up the thermostat and keep working. Lights, clocks, climate control—all insulate us from the natural cycles of days and seasons. The commodity day, for example, begins officially at midnight. The change is imperceptible: the skies have already been dark for hours and will be dark for hours more. So commodity days come and go like thieves in the night, with no one but the most dedicated clock-watchers to witness one day giving way to the next.

The Jewish calendar day, on the other hand, ends at nightfall, and its character varies with the seasons. In summer the days are longer, in winter shorter. How natural this is! When the temperatures are colder and life is harder, I need to hibernate more. Ordinarily we banish such considerations from our minds. But lighting candles on Friday afternoon close to sunset reminds us that it's the middle of December and night comes upon us early now. It restores us to the natural cycle of time. This is why we don't want to give up the rhythm of Shabbos and of our sacred calendar. They anchor us in the natural rhythm of things. In this postindustrial world we need to make a conscious decision to define times in which we will try to move in tandem with the cycles of mother nature. Otherwise we will spend all our days fighting her.

# ENSOULMENT

The Jewish story—the Torah—begins not with the first Jew or the first mitzvah but at the very dawn of creation. The first story in our Torah relates how God created the world in six days, "and on the seventh day," as the book of Exodus says later, "*shavat va-yinafash*, God rested and was refreshed" (Exodus 31:17). The Hebrew word *Shabbat,* more austere than *Shabbos,* gives us the sense of a laying down of tools, of entry into an absolute stillness. The word *yinafash,* often translated as "refreshed," is from the word *nefesh,* or soul, and literally means "became souled." God ceased all work on the seventh day, we are told, and was ensouled.

The biblical stories still echo in our mythic imaginations because they are vehicles of the deepest teachings. What deep teaching does this very first story of Torah convey? One of its messages, surely, is that a yin and yang of activity and rest are built into the very fabric of the universe. We see God laboring and recognize and honor the value of labor. And we witness God ceasing all work and taking time to rest and re-ensoul. One of the very first messages of Torah, then, is the crucial link between rest and reconnection to the deepest parts of ourselves. The story that we Jews tell ourselves, our children, and the world began and still begins with the Sabbath.

Why is this message so important? Because the Torah recognizes the power of all those practical tasks that clamor for our attention every day. It senses the danger that we will allow ourselves to be driven by our more material concerns and will never take the time to address the needs that arise at the deepest level of our being, the one we call "soul."

I want to tell you a story about the *meshuggeneh* Pinkas, "Crazy Pinkas." I spent one summer as a young man traveling in Central and South America collecting money for my alma mater, the Lubavitcher Yeshiva. I carried with me a bag containing a *shochet's* knife for ritual slaughtering and tools for fixing Torah scrolls, because I knew that in every town I came to—San Juan, Panama City, Balboa—there would be a *sefer Torah* that would need a little fixing. So I did my rounds. I relied on the goodwill of the community: my first question to the local Jews in every place I came to was: Where can I stay? And each time they would refer me to the one kosher Jew in San Juan or Costa Rica, the guy where all the Lubavitcher messengers would stay.

In this way I came to Managua, Nicaragua. Where should I stay? I asked. "With the *meshuggeneh* Pinkas," everybody said. They sent someone downtown with me to help me with the bags— help was very cheap in Managua in those days—and to take me to the store of *meshuggeneh* Pinkas. It was a dry goods and general store, where you could buy machetes and all kinds of things you might need in Nicaragua. The store was air-conditioned, and all the salesclerks understood English, which was a relief to me, and they were all extremely nice.

"Señor Pinkas? He is in the *officina*."

I said, "Would you please announce that I am here?"

The saleslady was polite but protective. Señor Pinkas comes in at eight o'clock in the morning, she told me. From eight to nine he does some business, then at nine o'clock he locks the door of his office and doesn't open it until eleven. He and his son spend that time studying the holy books, and nobody is admitted.

"What do you do if there is an emergency?" I asked.

"I knock on the door and give him a note," the lady replied, "and he can respond if he so wishes." So I asked her to please take my card and knock on the door and give it to him.

All of a sudden Pinkas comes out, side locks flying, beard, big *tzitzit* hanging out, a beautiful Jewish man. *"Sholom aleikhem, kimtz nur arein! Me halt in lernen in gemarah Gittin"*—we're in the middle of studying here, please sit down, we have a problem and perhaps you can help us." All this in the back of the most successful dry goods store in Managua. He was a marvelous human being.

So why was he called the *meshuggeneh* Pinkas? Because he was the only Jew in Managua who would insist on closing his store on Shabbos. Saturday was the big market day in Managua. People flocked from miles around to the *mercado central*. Even Jews did most of their business on Saturday—but *meshuggeneh* Pinkas had decided he was not going to open up on Shabbos.

For the first year or two he really struggled. Then word of this strange man got out to the local Seventh-day Adventists, and the minister came to speak with him. Somehow they managed to bridge their language gap. Pinkas, the minister pointed out, had a need for honest, polite, well-trained employees. The minister had just such a labor force in his church—and they didn't want to work on Shabbos either. This arrangement worked out wonderfully for both sides. Pinkas had far less produce pilfered by employees than anyone else in town. His Seventh-day Adventists got to rest on what was normally the busiest day of the week. And the store flourished. On Friday afternoons before they closed, Pinkas and his staff would prepare Saturday night bargains. People would be lined up with their donkeys to *shlep* home to their villages all the stuff they bought, waiting until after Shabbos was over, when Señor Pinkas and the Seventh-day Adventists would come and open up the *tienda* so they could do business.

So here was a person who sat and studied Torah for the best two hours of the day, who took the most lucrative business day off for rest and re-ensoulment, and who somehow made it all work. *Meshuggeneh* Pinkas! What a crazy guy!

TO MANY OF US, unfortunately, the idea of a traditional Shabbat conjures up more burden than benefit. Most of us heard a lot more about the "no-nos" than about the "yes" that Shabbos represents. If a child were to ask you, "What is Shabbat?" you might say, "It's the Jewish day of rest." If she persisted, "What do people do on that day?" you would probably start off by saying, "Well, there's all sorts of stuff you're not supposed to do." This is hardly surprising. A person who "keeps Shabbos," by traditional definition, does not drive, cook, or handle any form of money; use the telephone, TV, radio, computer, elevator, or anything else that requires electricity (except with the help of a preset timer or "Shabbos clock"); or carry anything outside the house (except in a city or area that has an *eruv,* or simulated wall around it). They might even use pretorn toilet paper to avoid the prohibition against tearing. This long list of restrictions is often what jumps out at us first when we think of Shabbos.

## WINDOW: THE RULES OF SHABBOS

What are the prohibitions of Shabbos, and where did they come from?

The Torah itself tells us little about how exactly the Sabbath is to be observed. "Six days shall you work and perform all your labors," Exodus 20:9 tells us. "And the seventh day shall be a sabbath of the Lord your God: you shall not do any work. . . . Because for six days God created the heavens and earth, the sea and all that's in it, and He rested on the seventh day. Therefore God blessed the seventh day and made it holy."

The word *Shabbat,* in its verb form, means "to cease and de- sist," and the rabbis defined thirty-nine acts to cease and desist from in keeping the Sabbath. Most of these fall into several broad categories. We are prohibited from all the activities that go into making bread, from plowing, sowing, and reaping to kneading and baking. Everything that has to do with producing clothes is forbidden, too, from shearing to dyeing, spinning, sewing, and weaving. Also off-limits were any of the acts that led to writing in those days, from skinning an animal's hide to scraping and tan- ning it to writing and erasing. We are forbidden, too, to build or destroy, kindle or extinguish a fire, or carry things outside the home. As society developed, later rabbis laid out further prohibitions, "descendants" of the original "father labors," designed to keep us from even approaching the forbidden acts themselves.

Various explanations are given for why these particular acts are the forbidden ones. The rabbis, noting how often Torah uses the word *melakhhah*, labor, to describe the work of building the *mishkan* or Tabernacle, defined the prohibited labors as those done in building the *mishkan*. More modern views have stressed that the prohibited activities were those by which our ancestors exhibited control and mastery over their world. We let go of this control, this mastery, on Shabbat so that we can just *be* and accept our world as it is. In thinking about how these prohibitions could be adjusted to bring about the Shabbos experience in our own lives, I think about the derivation of the word *melakhah*, which is from the root l-a-kh, to send. (Another derivative, *mal'akh*, means both messenger and angel, the one God sends.) For me, the actions we should avoid on Shabbos include those we would rather send someone else to do, delegatable work. But if weaving is where your passion is, rather than your business, and sitting down at your weaver's loom is what brings on the Shabbos experience for you, I have no problem with that.

Torah itself hints at the dual nature of Shabbat—the link between prohibition and benefit. Shabbat is number four of the Ten Commandments, listed in Exodus and repeated in Deuteronomy. Deuteronomy repeats nine of the commandments almost word for word, but the one about Shabbat has significant differences, beginning with the first word. Exodus 20:8 starts with the word *zakhor*—*remember* the Sabbath day. Deuteronomy 5:12 begins with the word *shamor*—*guard* the Sabbath Day. Why does Exodus have God saying "remember" while Deuteronomy records God as saying "guard"? Because, the rabbis tell us, when God gave the commandment, the two words were spoken simultaneously, in a single utterance. But because of the human inclination to make distinctions, some people heard the "guard"—the "no-nos"—and other people heard the "remember," the "yes." In order to make sure that both messages got through, Torah gives us both the "no" language and the "yes" language.

The prohibitions of Shabbos jump out at us first because anyone can understand a prohibition, whether they fulfill it or not. Modern Jews are inclined to resent such restrictions. On the other hand, I believe that to simply ignore them altogether is to risk tossing Shabbos out with the bathwater. The more we can get at the *spirit* of these laws, the more we can begin to grasp the benefits that Shabbos can bestow. Let's take a moment to imagine a world in which these prohibitions are taken for granted, as something that just comes with the territory. We can then begin to understand how refraining from certain actions and engaging in others in a Shabbos spirit might help us enter into a Shabbos space and sanctify whatever we choose to do on that day.

A traditional Shabbos is not a day to *do;* it is a day to *be.* No purchases are made, no business taken care of. We rest content with what we have. No long journeys are undertaken: wherever we are, we are content to be. The food has been prepared ahead of time, the arrangements have all been made. We are free to pamper our souls. We pray together, learn together, eat together, sing together, and invite our friends to join us as often as we can.

We express our love for one another and talk about things we've learned.

Imagine your spouse or partner rushes in and says, "Honey, listen, I got us tickets for an island vacation! It's a package deal. You pay up front: once we get there, everything is free. You're not going to believe this place. It has *no commercial establishments whatsoever.* There's nowhere to spend money! They don't allow any cars or mechanized vehicles on the island; everything is literally within walking distance. They ask the guests not to bring any cell phones, computers, TVs, or radios. We won't have to do any cooking: the meals are supposed to be great. 'So what do people *do?*' I asked the travel agent. 'Won't we go a little crazy, with so little stimulation?' She said, no, not at all, that people tend to get acclimated very quickly. You make a lot of friends, she said, and hang out together a lot, eating, taking walks. Often at mealtimes someone will start a song and everyone around the table joins in! You have a nap in the afternoon or do some meditation—it's just total downtime, total rejuvenation."

This description starts to get at what a traditional Shabbat can be about. This island exists, but you won't find it on the map. Even if we could, we wouldn't be able to afford it—especially as often as we need it! So we create this island in time instead.

Once we had a temple, the temple in Jerusalem. It was destroyed. We built another; that, too, was destroyed. At that point our whole underlying structure changed. We replaced that temple in space with what Rabbi Abraham Joshua Heschel imagined as a holy temple in time, a temple in which to build and sustain a connection with the Infinite, a temple that we consecrate by conscious acts of will. That temple is the Sabbath.

The Hasidic masters of the Pshischa lineage, in particular, saw this process as part of a vast three-stage evolution. Following the ancient Kabbalistic work known as the *Sefer Yetzirah* (Book of Creation), they called these stages *olam* (world), *shanah* (year), and *nefesh* (soul). We started in *olam*, in the world of space, of physical coordinates. This world gave us the laws that had to do with space, with the Holy Temple. From there we moved into *shanah*, time, where we started to elaborate the many laws connected with Shabbos, our sanctuary in time. This helps us begin to understand why the Shabbos laws are so abundant. We no longer have the Temple sacrifices; what we offer up to God instead is our time. In the third stage, we will move into *nefesh*, the realm of the spirit, of inner human experience. This is a very exciting vision, one that imagines Judaism as deepening and evolving, rather than remaining static and continuously harking back to bygone days. A Shabbos in the world of *nefesh*, of deep re-ensoulment, is, I believe, where we're going now. This is the YES of Shabbat practice that we have to seek.

## WINDOW:
## THE EVOLUTION OF SHABBOS

Just as an individual Shabbos practice gathers "soul mass" over time, so did the Jewish people take time to build the Sabbath. The development of the Sabbath idea probably didn't really get going until around the time of Ezra the Scribe in the very late biblical period. True, the instruction to institute a day of rest is set out clearly in the Ten Commandments. Other places in the Pentateuch add a handful of prohibitions and the right animals to sacrifice and instruments to play. But we hear very little more about Shabbos from the time we entered Canaan and all the way through the First Temple period. The books of Joshua, Judges, Samuel, and Kings barely mention the Sabbath at all! Had the Sabbath been imagined right off the bat as the beautiful and sanctified space that it later became, we would expect to find more psalms praising it, for example. In fact we find only a single psalm to the Sabbath, Psalm 92. Only when we get to Isaiah do we start to get a sense of the delight that Shabbat can represent:

*If because of Shabbos, my sacred day,*
*you will stop toiling for your wants,*
*and instead, honor it, arousing Shabbos delight,*
*desisting from your errands—from seeking bargains*
*and making deals on my sacred day;*
*then you will delight in Yah,*
*and I will seat you on top of the world,*
*and nourish you with the inheritance of Jacob.*
*This is what Yah has promised.*

—ISAIAH 58:13–14

Lift yourself above the restrictions, Isaiah seems to be saying. Delight in the rest that the Sabbath brings. Shabbat is not a time to think of scarcity but of abundance—an abundance not of worldly gain but of deeper and more transcendent joy. "Honor it," not in the sense of a chore, but as you would honor a promise, out of a sense of love and of doing the right thing. Do that, God promises, and "I will seat you on top of the world."

The basic prohibitions of the Five Books of Moses were only filled out much later, at the time of the Mishnah. In most cases the rabbis greatly expanded the prohibitions in their desire to guard the Sabbath from any profane activity. Our relationship to fire is an exception. The verse in the Torah, "Do not burn any fires in all your dwellings on the Sabbath day" (Exodus 35:3), not only forbids the *lighting* of a flame; it seems to forbid any flame at all to continue burning on Shabbat. But the rabbis realized that little Sabbath joy would be found in houses plunged in darkness, so they used the authority Torah gave them to interpret the law for their own times. The prohibition against kindling or maintaining fire on Shabbat would stand, the rabbis decreed. But henceforth we would light two candles to bring in the Sabbath, so we could sit and eat and sing together by their light. The flames we kindle to bring in Shabbos and festivals are the last fire sacrifices we have in our lives.

Later Jewish teachings added a whole layer of spirituality to the terse biblical references and rabbinical prohibitions. A mystical teaching that dates back to rabbinic times, and that was strongly underscored in the *Zohar,* the central work of Kabbalah, is that we receive on Shabbos a *neshamah yeterah.* The simple translation of this would be "an additional soul," but that doesn't quite capture it: "additional" feels like quantity, as if on Shabbos we got two pieces of gefilte fish instead of one. That is not what is meant here. *Neshamah yeterah* really means a superabundance of soul, an overflowing. During the week we are very much into driving our physical bodies. On Shabbos, we give our bodies pleasure and a rest so we can become transparent to *nefesh*, to soul.

On Shabbos we move to a higher plane. To say that I have a *neshamah yeterah* is to focus on an additional quality of consciousness that I usually don't have access to. When meditation teachers say, "See what is arising, follow your breath, and see what comes up," what they are saying is, become transparent: instead of staying in your head, become transparent to what is happening. This, too, gives a sense of what is meant here. By carving out a Sabbath in time I can begin to explore questions like: What happens when I don't have any striving? What are the feelings that fill me? By taking some restrictions upon myself and limiting my needs, I can begin to see what happens when I don't need anything. I can begin to hook into a place where everything I have is right here, where all is good. The transparency to the universe that comes from that place, the feeling that we are embraced by and integral to the universe— that is the *neshamah yeterah,* the overflowing of soul. We rise to a higher spiritual level. Our horizons get bigger. Just as they say, "On a clear day you can see forever," so the more transparent we become the farther we can really see.

## ENTERING THE SABBATH STATE

How, then, can we achieve the Sabbath state? Can we taste something of the essence of Shabbat without necessarily following the laws that the tradition lays down?

The first step toward a Sabbath practice is to simply set aside some time to sit quietly without distraction—to stop doing and simply BE. This in itself can be very hard for us. We Jews once had a saying that a city without ten loafers—by which we mean contemplatives—isn't a real city at all. But today we find it almost unbearable to sit and do nothing for even a half hour! We have a great deal going on in our lives, we might be the caregivers for our families, but Shabbos just can't happen if we don't take an island of time to ourselves. We don't need to wait until Shabbos itself to do this. In our day, when the pressures of the weekday have mounted, mini-Sabbaths during the week—daily if possible—have become a psychological necessity. The traditional Jew, too, would snatch moments of repose from workday life for entering the calming presence of God through prayer, creating a daily piece of Shabbos in that midweek space.

Time, in this great and unequal society of ours, is the great equalizer. When a census was taken of the Children of Israel who came out of Egypt, the people were asked to give a half shekel each; "the rich shall not give more, nor the poor less." This same spirit is true today with time. A half hour dedicated to re-ensoulment rewards rich and poor alike. Our dedication of time for this purpose is itself a holy act: in Hebrew the word for dedicate, *le-kaddesh,* is the same word for sanctify, from the root *kaddosh,* holy.

So begin by sitting. Don't meditate, don't pray, just take some time to rest in a place of "I don't want anything, and I don't fear anything. I have no aversion, and I have no attraction. I'm not pushing anything, and I'm not pulling anything. I'm just here." Sit with an open heart, feel your connection with that sacred presence in the universe, and say, "Compassionate One, here I am." Sit with that for a while and see what comes up in your heart and in your mind. If some thoughts come in, welcome them and remember them. If some words want to come out, let them out. If you want, keep a journal, later on, of what comes to you.

Or you might begin by saying, "Dear God, whoever and whatever you are, I'm in the service of the greatest good for myself, for my family, and for the world. If there are any orders for me today, I'm ready to take them." And then sit quietly and see what comes. At first what comes to you will probably be something like, "Bring that book back to the library" or "Make sure the car is serviced." But the more you encourage these things to come in for you, the more they will refine themselves. It's as if there's a little water seeping from the ground, and you begin to dig, and pretty soon you have a real spring there because you have removed all the debris. It will flow a lot better for you after a while, but it takes steadiness. Better to do it intermittently than not at all, but if you want to domesticate your relationship with God so that you can count on it, as we can count on the harvest of a crop we plant and tend carefully, then that takes time.

Just as we light candles to bring in the Sabbath, so candles can be very helpful during a mini-Sabbath as well. You can do this even during the week. The aura of a candle defines a sacred space; the life span of that flame defines a sacred time. Light the candle and then bring the light in to yourself. That's the gesture that Grandma used to make with her hands when she lit candles on Shabbos—waving the light in, calling it into her heart. Close your eyes and see it burning in your heart, and then send out your prayer, your aspiration.

Let your attention be the wick—
your dedication the fuel—
your soul the flame—
rising and falling, rising and falling, reaching for that presence.

Or you might listen to some favorite music that you otherwise wouldn't have a chance to listen to. This, too, is a kind of prayer that we can offer to God. As you appreciate the music, make room for God in your rejoicing. You might say something like, "I offer my appreciation of this music as a gift to you, and thank you for keeping me company when it's over." Nothing more complicated than that.

Or just sit and think of all the things you're grateful for, close your eyes and send out a kind of quiet "I appreciate that, God," and see where that alone will take you.

All these are simple ways in which we can get some Sabbath into our lives. You may do a Sabbath like this and it won't do anything for you. The next might not either. But after a while it starts to work. The way practices like these can gently wear away the instincts to go, go, GO! that we've built up over a lifetime— that is what the traditional teachings were getting at. Spend half an hour in that clean and peaceful place of "God rested and was ensouled." This will open the door.

## FRIDAY NIGHT: WELCOMING THE BRIDE

Most people who celebrate Shabbat in any way do something on Friday night: lighting candles, perhaps saying blessings over wine and challah, sitting down to a special meal with the family.

So let's spend some time talking about the hours in which we first welcome Shabbos into our home.

The word *Shabbat* in Hebrew is feminine: a loving, joyful, nurturing word. The traditional Friday night prayers speak of welcoming the Sabbath bride. She comes to us at dusk, that special time that is imbued with the qualities of consciousness of both day and night. The Jewish day usually begins only when the light has fully faded and darkness is complete, but by tradition we bring Shabbat in about a half hour early, as if unable to restrain ourselves from running to greet her. The followers of the Kabbalist Isaac Luria, the Lion of Safed, would go out into the fields or the synagogue courtyard singing, "Come, beloved friend, let's meet the bride, let's greet the Shabbat"—a song that is central to the Friday night service to this day.

Friday night, to me, conjures up homecoming, as if coming in out of the cold into a warm house, your eyeglasses steaming up, greeting your family, "Good Shabbos! Ah, I can smell the soup, the fish." The Jewish home is filled with the aromas of God's cornucopia, telling of an abundance that is greater than all our needs, real or imagined. We feel loved and cared for, and our workday worries begin to fall away. On Friday evening, a traditional Jew who may have run frantically all week long could finally put down the burdens of the week and say, "At last! Thank God. Now I am free just to sit and enjoy. I don't need to run. I don't need to make, do, fix, or change. For today, I can just *be.*" Even the deepest knots loosen up.

Our Sabbath is the last day of the week, not the first, and this is important. Celebrating the Sabbath on the first day would be like saying, "I'm resting up on Shabbos so I can work the rest

of the week." Instead, the first six days of the week lead us to
Shabbos, as if to say, "I'm doing all my doing so I can have some
BE-ing."

Shabbos gives a rhythm to our entire week. The traditional
*davening* (liturgy) begins to whisper of the Sabbath's arrival as
early as Wednesday morning. After Wednesday's "psalm of the
day," Psalm 94, worshippers would add the first three verses of
Psalm 95, which are the verses that begin the Friday night service:
"Come, let us sing to Yah, let us make a joyful clamoring. . . .
Let us come before Yah's presence with thanksgiving." You get
the sense of, "Only two more days till Shabbos," of getting
closer and ever closer to that sanctuary in time.

Come Friday we begin our preparations in earnest. As the
hour nears, if we take the time seriously, things begin to heat up.
Everyone who has been involved in Shabbos has felt the rush of
Friday afternoon as the flywheel of time speeds toward the appointed hour. Even in June, when the days are longest, we never
have enough time to get everything together for Shabbos. All
the family members rush around, cleaning house, preparing food,
setting the table, getting washed up and changed, working up a
sweat.

Once Shabbos starts to become important to us, we begin to
understand this sense of breathless anticipation and preparation.
Imagine a colleague is due for dinner at six o'clock. By five-thirty
everything is already set up and you don't fix anything anymore.
You're ready. But what happens when your lover is supposed to
come for dinner? I want to give it so much. I want the atmosphere to be so delightful. How would it be if I put a flower
here? Could I do a special decoration? Let me fold the napkins

in a special way. That is how it is with Shabbos. I never feel that
I have enough time. I can always think of something else to do
to welcome the queen. The final touches that we make in preparation for this love encounter are so important. When at last the
candles are lit and we greet our lovely guest with that first
"Shabbat Shalom" or "Good Shabbos"—then all the rising tension of Friday afternoon can finally find release.

The Friday night *kiddush,* or blessing over the wine, begins
with the words *yom ha-shishi va-yekhulu ha-shamayim.* These four
consecutive words from Genesis actually come from two different chapters. The first two words, "the sixth day," are the closing words of chapter 1, in which the world is created. The latter
two words, "Completed were the skies," are the first words of
chapter 2, in which God rests from the labor of creation. A mystic
interpretation points out that only on Shabbos does the acronym
of these four words—YHVH—become joined together to complete the holy name of God.

## QUALITY TIME

Judaism is often called a householder religion. We perform our
rites, rituals, and prayers among family and friends. We have no
monastic tradition, which can rob the community of its most
enlightened members. Renunciation of worldly concerns is dis-
couraged: even the sages were instructed to learn a trade and have
a family. Our emphasis on family and community is something
of which we can be justly proud, and nowhere is it more true
than on Shabbos.

Be sure to hurry home from synagogue on Friday night, the
sages instructed, lest a family member fall asleep and miss the
Shabbos meal. Kabbalistic and Hasidic sources interpreted the prohibition against fire to include anger as well, and urged husbands
and wives to set aside their quarrels and let harmony reign on
Shabbos. On Friday night, by ancient custom, we also place our
hands on our children's heads and bless them.

However you interpret it, Shabbos is quintessentially a family practice, for there is no better way to enrich your family life
than to take a break from all the usual distractions and spend
some "quality time" together. Even small children will welcome
the idea of setting aside time to relax and be together. Almost
every aspect of a traditional Friday night carries a lot of experience
that can appeal to a child: dressing up, lighting candles, gathering as a family, inviting guests, singing, sipping wine from the
kiddush cup, special food—and special desserts.

Be creative! Creativity is so important in nurturing a love of
Shabbos in our children, a love they will later be able to draw upon
in meeting the pressures of adult life. Some of us remember
how hard it was to be pushed into Shabbos in ways that bored
us. When I was a teenager I remember resenting Shabbos afternoons. Papa made all of us take a Shabbos nap. But I didn't feel
like taking a nap: I wanted to be out with my friends! Only years
later, when I was already working during the week as a furrier
or a diamond cutter or whatever I did at that time, I realized the
importance of the lesson my father was trying to impart. How
do you begin to instill an enthusiasm for Shabbos in a child who
is not old enough to know that he needs relief from the week?

When my kids were too young to go to shul on Friday evening, we used to have what we called "five minuteses." Each child had five minutes before we lit the candles to offer whatever they wanted to the Shabbos celebration. My daughter Shalvi, who at that time was in love with *The Wizard of Oz,* would sing "Somewhere Over the Rainbow." Barya wanted us to sing "Follow the Leader" and follow him around. My son Yotam would say "Zizik!" meaning "music," whereupon I would put on "The Happy Moog," his favorite piece, and he would dance hopsy-dopsy on a little trampoline we had in the room. Then the kids would chorus, "Ya, ya, we know what Abba wants. He wants five minutes' quiet!" But they loved the sense of control over their "five minuteses," of each having something to contribute.

When the kids got older we had the custom of sitting down on Friday afternoon and writing each other Shabbos love letters. After the blessings over the wine and the challah on Friday night, one of the children would take the letters around. Routine can take over in such a terrible way when you're living together; this gave us a wonderful way to tell each other what really mattered.

## DOORWAY:
## CREATING SHABBOS IN YOUR HOME

The deep psychological and spiritual insight of Shabbos is one of our tradition's great treasures. Our modern contributions are flexibility and creativity, which I believe are more important at this point than the rigidity around Shabbos that the tradition can sometimes display. We need to bring a process of experimentation to augment the wisdom of *halakhah* (law). In the Saturday morning kiddush we say *"Ve-shamru venei Yisrael et ha-Shabbat le-dorotam"* (Let the children of Israel keep the Shabbos for [the benefit of] the generations). Creating a Shabbos, in other words—and creating a Shabbos that our next generation will want to pass on to their children—is *in our hands.* There are all sorts of ways to bring our practice of Shabbos alive. Engage as many senses as you can.

*Clothing.* When we divest ourselves of our weekly garments, the Kabbalists taught, we should intend to cast from ourselves the otherness in which we dwell most of the time. When we put on our Shabbos garments we then draw upon ourselves an additional level of holiness.

The lawyer or broker who wears jeans on the Sabbath is making a statement about resting. He has taken off his professional role and donned clothes in which he can loaf at his ease. Others might put on special garb to enhance the delight of heart, mind, and soul. A combination of comfort and ease with a little bit of ritual or flair can help us move into a wonderful space. Under the right circumstances a "Garden of Eden" Shabbos with no clothes at all could be an amazing way of "Shabbosing."

*Food.* A favorite song sings of the "quail and fish" consumed on Shabbos—even though the shtetl poor could probably afford nothing of the kind. We might choose to give our stomachs a Sabbath from processed foods by way of celebration, to enjoy a day of uncooked fruits and vegetables and juices during the summer months. Health permitting, this would certainly be a great time to indulge in that dessert we've been denying ourselves all week.

Shabbos is a time of plenty. As you raise the food to your lips, try to feel as if God were feeding you directly, or as if you yourself were feeding the Shabbos bride. Our souls, in their superabundance that we receive on this day, become the Shabbos bride at that point.

*Fragrances.* The Jews of Yemen and other Sephardim had the custom to prepare fragrant flowers and herbs for Shabbos. Maybe Mom could have a special scent for Friday evening that would carry over to Shabbos morning. Breathing in the Sabbath through our very nostrils, associating wonderful smells with the Sabbath celebration, can be a very powerful thing.

I once held the post of "religious environmentalist" at Camp Rama, a camp run by the Conservative movement in Connecticut. One of my goals was to transmit to the kids some of the sensory, nonverbal values and experiences that go into the adjective *Shabbosdik*. Every Friday, for example, as the kids were dressing for Shabbat and the special Friday night meal was cooking in the kitchen, we would take all the fans we had and set them up to blow the smell of the food all over the camp, to permeate the air with the anticipation of Shabbat. I felt that linking nonverbal experiences to the social and other pleasures of Shabbat would store these experiences in a much deeper place than just verbal explanations, a place that would bring them back to these experiences later in life.

*Music and other media.* The traditional Friday night prayer for welcoming the Sabbath is full of references to song. Psalm 95: "Come, let us sing to God . . . let us call out songs of praise." Psalm 92: "A song for the Sabbath day. It is good to thank God, to sing the praise of your name. . . . Upon ten-stringed instrument

and lyre, with singing accompanied by harp." Rabbinic law pro-
hibits the playing of even nonelectronic instruments on Shabbos
for arcane reasons. But a person who loves playing music but is not
a professional musician, who only on Shabbos can find the time
to sit down—maybe with friends—and offer a song or a tune in
honor of Shabbos, is celebrating the day in a way that the liturgy
itself suggests. Taking the time to listen to the symphony we never
have time for during the week, and to listen with the express purpose of welcoming and enjoying the Sabbath and transcending
the everyday, is to me a quintessentially Shabbosdik activity.

Best of all is to make all our preparations for such activities
ahead of time, so that all we have to do on Shabbos is to soak it
in and enjoy. I once brought a record of Leonard Bernstein's
*Chichester Psalms* to the house of an Orthodox rabbi where I was
to spend Shabbat. As we agreed, I switched on his amplifier and
his turntable before the candles were lit, so that I didn't have to
violate the Sabbath by completing any electrical circuits. All I had
to do was put the needle on. After the Friday night service and
Shabbat dinner we sat down to listen to the music. Before we
started I recited *"yishtabach shimkha,"* a paean of praise from the
morning prayers: "Thank you, God, for song and hymn and an-
them." The rabbi loved the music and appreciated the blessing.
He himself would not repeat it, he said, though he could find no
fault in my procedure. "But," he added, "I thank you for giving
me this experience."

There are a whole series of movies, albums, and other things
that could be shared. Imagine sitting with the kids and watching

a comedy like *The Frisco Kid,* about a Polish rabbi (Gene Wilder) in the Wild West! We need not resort to any media at all: dancing and singing are part of the traditional repertoire, especially among Hasidim.

And so, of course, is silence.

*Bath.* Taking a bath or shower before Shabbos to wash the week out of our hair has a special significance. In very religious circles adults would go to immerse themselves in the *mikveh,* or ritual bath, on Friday afternoon. This immersion, the *Zohar* tells us, makes visible the additional aura that Shabbos bestows on us. Simply washing our face with both hands, Kabbalists believed, revealed the image of God that the week normally obscures in our visage. Not everyone has time to immerse themselves in some way before Shabbos, however. On Shabbos, too, we can imagine family members gathering in a hot tub, sharing their week, clearing away any *shmutz* that has accumulated in the air, forgiving one another and relaxing with one another, washing away the week.

*Sex.* Tradition makes no secret of it: sex on Shabbos is a mitzvah. A loving couple who make sure to take their time enacting our union with the *Shekhinah,* the feminine face of God, and doing so lavishly and tenderly, are celebrating Shabbat in the most wonderful way. I once got into a conversation about masturbation with a bar-mitzvah boy I was teaching. Try waiting until Shabbos comes around, I suggested, and don't be a stranger from God; make sure to let God into it.

*Other soul-nourishing activities.* Save up for Shabbos those activities that pamper your soul. Here I would take a more lenient approach

toward certain activities that traditional *halakhah* forbids, as long
as they are done in the spirit of Shabbos. If you enjoy gardening
for its own sake, rather than regard it as a chore you'd just as soon
delegate to someone else; if you're enjoying spending time with
your plants rather than working on a crop with which to feed your
family, then gardening is a Shabbosdik activity for you. If you're
a computer programmer by trade but a potter at heart, and if setting aside some Shabbos time each week would allow you to enjoy
sitting down at the potter's wheel, then pottery is a Shabbosdik
activity for you.

We might swear off the telephone during our Shabbos celebration—nothing can intrude on a Shabbos like a telemarketing
call!—but have a special signal for family and friends (or simply
use caller ID). A friend of mine used to have a telephone date on
Shabbos afternoon with a woman he was engaged to, who lived
in another city, and the first thing they'd discuss was their
thoughts on the Torah portion of the week. The telephone becomes a sacred instrument when it allows us to do things like this.

Spiritual gains should not come at emotional expense. Trying any
new activity can rock the family boat at first. Discuss these issues
beforehand to prepare the ground, and start small. Go at a pace
that everyone can handle. Developing re-ensoulment skills takes
time.

# ADVANCED PRACTICE: THE DIFFERENT
# FLAVORS OF SHABBOS

We have already gotten the sense that a regular Sabbath practice can offer us far more than simply twenty-four hours of nonactivity. The buildup to Shabbos can enrich the entire rhythm of our week. And the Sabbath day itself, as it progresses from Friday to Saturday night, traditionally contains within itself at least four distinct atmospheres: Friday night, Shabbos morning, Shabbos afternoon, and Saturday night.

### Shabbos Morning: Resting in the Shabbos Moment

On Friday afternoon the lover we have been parted from all week approaches. We rush to prepare everything for her arrival, until finally the tension of Friday is released in our joyful and passionate union on Friday night.

On Saturday morning we rise together in a calmer mood. If on Friday night we welcome Shabbos with the feeling of, "Oy, was that a heavy week," and on Shabbos afternoon we start feeling, "Oy, am I going to miss you, how am I going to get through the week to come?" then Shabbos morning is our time for being in the Shabbos moment. We're not recovering from the previous week; we're not starting to think about the next; we're just totally immersed in the spirit of Shabbos.

On Shabbos morning we rest in the feeling that "the universe is unfolding as it should," in the famous phrase of Max Ehrmann's

"Desiderata." During the week we run around, trying, each in our own small way, to make a better world, but on Shabbos morning we embrace a world that doesn't need any fixing, a world that is perfect in itself. It is a more cerebral time, a good time take a step back and see all of creation "under the aspect of eternity," in philosopher Baruch Spinoza's phrase, to reconnect to the eternal truths of our lives, those truths that rise above changing circumstances.

Some of us go to synagogue regularly; many others go more occasionally, for bar mitzvahs or the High Holy Days. The central part of the Sabbath morning service is the Torah reading, which, in contrast to the more emotional appeal of Friday night, deals a lot more with the conceptual, intellectual side of the soul. Sometimes the reading engages us more—the stories of Genesis, the saga of the Exodus—while the arcane details of the tabernacle and sacrificial cult might engage us less. One way to connect more closely to the text than merely hearing it read out loud is to join one of the many study groups that meet Shabbos morning at an increasing number of synagogues. There you will find people—many of them beginners—delving more deeply into some part of the weekly portion, focusing less on an analysis of text and commentaries than on trying to unpack what the text has to say to us today, to the lives we are leading, to our minds and hearts.

Like the Friday night service, the morning service is traditionally followed by kiddush over a cup of wine, made either when we get home from synagogue, or sometimes in synagogue, with our family gathered around us. The Shabbat morning kiddush is more flexible than the one on Friday night: the rabbis prescribed some verses to say before the the blessing *"borei peri ha-gofen"* (who created the fruit of the vine), but we can vary those verses if we wish. I love the clarity of the "sitting on top of the world" quote from Isaiah (58:13–14), so I say that, but add whatever speaks to you. Maybe a friend or family member wants to offer a short, free-verse poem, and you could begin with that.

Around the lunch table—again, by tradition—we sing songs. In contrast to the more somber songs that we sing as Shabbat nears its end, these are happy songs, songs praising God or the Shabbat itself. Many of the tunes are lighthearted: one recent favorite making the rounds has been to sing *"Deror Yikra"* (Let Freedom Be Proclaimed)—a complex and beautiful poem by the medieval poet and grammarian Dunash ben Labrat of Baghdad—to the tune of "Sloop John B." Others are sung with deeper feeling. Another good thing to do is to tell stories: some fine collections exist, such as those of Peninnah Schram, Howard Schwartz, Nina Jaffe, or Barbara Diamond Goldin. You might choose to read a story every week, or to have one of your kids read it and get people to respond to it.

## Shabbos Afternoon: The Hour of Yearning

As the shadows get longer on Shabbos afternoon, the hour draws near when we must part again from our beloved for six long days. In Hasidic circles we would gather in the fading light for *shaleshudes,* the third of the three meals that tradition urges us to enjoy on Shabbos. Since the midday meal was but a recent memory, the food would be sparse, but the feeling of fellowship was strong. We would sing together melodies of longing and love for Shabbos and for God, like "Oh, how I long for the light of the Shabbos" and "You who love my soul." The feeling in the room was, "Oy, Shabbos is so good. If only it could be like this for the entire world. When will the *yom she-kulo Shabbat,* the day that is altogether Shabbos, arrive? When will the messianic time be here?"

Shaleshudes, says the Kotzker Rebbe, is that hour of which the Rabbis spoke when they said, "Better an hour in repentance and good deeds in this world than all of life in the next world." For as you sat and sang these songs of yearning, feeling that all too soon the extra dimension of soul you'd been given would flee before the cares of the coming week, you would sigh and be washed over with the longing to lead a good and moral life. "Oy, Master of the Universe, I need to be better, I need to be holier, I need to be . . ." Hasidim refer to Shabbat as *me'eyn olam ha-ba,* a taste of the world to come. They believe that the soul, that spark of the Divine within us, is not bound by the restrictions of time and space and therefore can visualize perfections that have not yet been manifested in this world. This is what allows us on Shabbos to visit a time not yet come and to envision futures as yet unrealized. Shabbos helps us make the holy real.

There is no better way to celebrate the waning hours of Shabbos than with a group of friends, particularly if they can enter with you into such a Shabbosdik space. Why not invite people over, sing some songs, listen to a beautiful piece of music together, have a meaningful conversation? These are wonderful moments to try to envision the kind of world we want for ourselves and our children—not necessarily as the subject of the conversation, but as a thread that runs through it. The time that

we spend together in the fading light can be transformative, helping to form within us the resolution to help in some small way
to build the world that we yearn for in the coming week.

## Havdalah: The Moment of Separation

When the sky is dark and three stars are visible, we part from the
Sabbath and begin our week with the *Havdalah* (separation) ceremony. Saying good-bye to our Sabbath, however we celebrated
and understood it, is very important. Declaring the boundaries
of our sanctuary in time helps us retain its blessings. Normally
we go from one consciousness to another without giving the
matter much thought. How many times have we returned from
vacation, only to have our tranquillity go up in smoke during
our first frantic hours at work? Or imagine you have a sweet,
sweet union with your lover: you feel as if you were one body,
one mind, one heart. Then, the next day, you have a fight. We are
sometimes tempted in such cases to dismiss the sweet memories
of the night before. How could we be having this terrible fight
now if that union had really been real? Havdalah affirms that,
no, Shabbos is Shabbos, and the week is the week; the reality of
Shabbos is true for Shabbos; the reality of the week is true for
the week. Rabbi Abraham Joshua Heschel saw Havdalah as the
kiddush for the week—the sanctification of the secular.

Perhaps no Jewish ceremony engages more senses in a shorter
time than Havdalah. (The text can be found in any prayer book.)
We first make a blessing over wine, which we will pass around at
the end of Havdalah so everyone can have a sip. We deliberately
pour an overflowing cup, spilling some wine into the plate, to

symbolize that blessing, that overflow of Shabbos that we want to take with us going forward. Next we make a blessing over a box of *b'samim,* fragrant spices, such as cinnamon or cloves. Some interpretations compare this to a lover who, before she departs for the week, leaves us a letter dabbed with her perfume, a sweet remembrance of her presence. Another tradition says that the scent serves to revive us as our additional soul departs from us. The third blessing is on a traditional braided candle, which children love to hold. Fire, the midrash tells us, was created on the first Shabbos night. Just as fire can be used to build or to destroy, so can we choose to use the coming week for good or for ill. We end with the blessing of Havdalah itself, recognizing the distinctions that God built into the universe.

After Havdalah is over we douse the candle in the spilled wine, bringing together the wine and the light. In my community we would then dip our fingers into the wine and touch them to our eyes and our pockets, so some of the blessing of Shabbos would overflow into our week. As the mystical *Zohar* says, "From it [the Sabbath] all days are blessed." We wanted "remember the Sabbath day" to be something that happens every day!

## Saturday Night

Everybody loves Saturday night. In much of the world, thanks to the Christian Sabbath, the kids can even stay up late and get a chance to appreciate it, too. A Saturday night celebration can be the best vehicle to take the tranquillity of Shabbos into the week.

Hasidic communities often hold a *melaveh malkah,* or "es-

corting of the queen," on Saturday night after Shabbos is out.
Just as the followers of the Ari walked out to greet the Sabbath
bride, so do we accompany her on her departure as far as we
can. The melaveh malkah, too, has traditional songs—sometimes accompanied by instruments, now that Shabbat is over.
And we tell stories, too, especially stories of the Baal Shem Tov,
the founder of Hasidism. Hasidim love the stories of the Besh"t
and his wonders, but the stories that are told Saturday night are
not so much the wonder-working stories, but ones about ordinary people who exerted themselves in the direction of extraordinary virtue. I remember the very first story I heard at a
melaveh malkah. It went something like this.

One day the Baal Shem Tov sits at his table with his people.
The weather is getting cold, but he says, "Get the wagon together,
and make sure you bring some *lekach* and some *bronfen* (cake and
spirits), and come with me." So they get into the wagon, and after
a time they come to an inn. The Baal Shem says to the innkeeper,
"Can you prepare for a wedding?"

And the innkeeper says, "Yes, of course. How many people?"

"Not too many people," the Baal Shem replied, "but we'll
need a nice meal."

"No problem," the innkeeper says. "I'll send over to another
fellow who has a roadhouse a little bit further on, so he and his
wife can come and help. I'm a little bit short-staffed right now,"
he explains. "I usually have a young woman and a young man
here to help me, but they're off today, the two of them."

"Where did they go?" the Baal Shem says.

"Well, they're about to get married, and today they went to

the town to buy what they'll need for their new home together. They've been saving up for years."

"Very good," the Baal Shem Tov says. "All right, start preparing."

Meanwhile, the young couple are on their way to town. No sooner do they get to the market when they see a family being dragged through the streets in chains. The town crier shouts in front of them, "These people haven't paid the rent to the landlord! They are going to be put into the darkest jail until they rot there and die!"

The couple are appalled. "How much do they owe?" they ask the town crier.

"Three hundred rubles," he says.

Three hundred rubles! It is all they have. But he looks at her and she looks at him, and yes, they take off their money belts and give everything they have to redeem the family. Before the family have even recovered enough to thank them, the couple are gone.

On their way back, they agree: "We can't tell the people that we gave away all our hard-earned money: they'll call us fools! Let's rough each other up a little, and when we get back we'll say that robbers fell on us and took our money."

So they come back bruised and empty-handed to find the inn in an uproar, preparing for a wedding as the Baal Shem had requested. The innkeeper rushes up and says, "Good, you're here! Quick, I need help setting up the—oy, vey, what happened to you? Where's the furniture?" And they tell him the whole tale of woe.

At this, the Baal Shem Tov calls them both aside and says, "It's your wedding that we're preparing for, and I am here to marry you myself." And so they are married.

Now, it was the custom that the guests at the wedding would say a *droshe geshank,* a little speech announcing the present that each guest is giving to the couple. "I give a pair of handsome brass candlesticks," one of the innkeepers says. "I'm going to give a baking trough," says the other. At some point they turn to the Baal Shem. "What about you, rabbi?"

And the Baal Shem says, "To the groom, I give the estate of Count Pototzki. To the bride, I give the Countess Pototzki's jewelry."

All the guests laugh uproariously and they continue with their meal and the seven traditional blessings.

Suddenly, before dessert is on the table, the Baal Shem says to the couple, "You must leave now, right away. Get on your wagon and horse and go."

"Where should we go?"

"Into the forest. Go."

In the meantime a snowstorm has started, a blizzard. The couple are in the middle of the forest and lose their way. All of a sudden, the horse rears up and refuses to go a step farther. When they peer ahead to see what the problem is, they see the body of a young boy lying in the snow. They dismount quickly and pick him up. He's still alive, and they rub him all over and give him some schnapps and the *lekach* that the Baal Shem Tov gave them for the way.

"Who are you?" they ask the boy. "Where are your parents?"

"I am the son of the Count and Countess Pototzki," the boy tells them. "I received a new horse for my birthday, but the

horse threw me off and I don't remember anything after that."
And he points them to the castle of the count.

Meanwhile the count and his wife are beside themselves with
worry. The horse they'd bought for their son had returned without its rider. The count's followers had been unable to find the
boy in the worsening storm, and the weather was getting so bad
that they were afraid to continue. Finally, in desperation, the
count says, "I pledge my entire estate to the person who brings
back my son!"

"And I pledge my jewelry as well!" says the countess.

Just then the couple arrives with the boy on their horse. And
that's how the Baal Shem's *drosha geshank* to that couple, who
had given all their money away to redeem that captive family,
came to pass.

My friend Shlomo Carlebach of blessed memory would tell
these stories so well that I'd call him the master of "virtuous reality." After one of his stories you would walk away wishing you
could have a moment like that hero who gave it all away. Nor
did this remain in the realm of theory with him. I know of at
least one occasion in which Shlomo signed over a substantial
check he'd just received for one of his concerts to a person who
came to him in need of help.

Embedded in all these tales was the message that any one of
us, with no warning or preparation, may be presented with the
opportunity to serve as the Holy One's instrument to improve
the world—*if* we rise to the occasion. This vision, this mystic
ideal, this high ambition, is what we take forward with us into
the week.

# MESSAGE TO THE WORLD

Our ideal picture of the Sabbath is one in which not just Jews but the whole world can find deep rest and re-ensoulment. At the *Oneg Shabbat* (literally "Shabbat joy," or Sabbath party) at the Peretz shul where I lived in Winnipeg, members of the Arbeter Ring (Workmen's Circle) used to sing *"Zoll zine Shabbos oyf der Welt"* (Let there be Shabbos in the whole world). The Arbeter Ring was an organization dedicated to Yiddish culture and socialist values rather than to any religious practice. But as unionists who fought for better conditions for workers everywhere, they clearly subscribed to the idea of a Shabbos as an inalienable right of all people.

Once, in the early sixties, I was presiding over a Sabbath celebration for B'nai B'rith in Estes Park, Colorado. By the time Shabbos came in, the wide open spaces of Colorado had started to speak to me, and I sang the kiddush to the tune of "Home On the Range." A few people giggled, but most of them understood. I wanted the kiddush to resonate with the feeling of "Where seldom is heard a discouraging word, and the skies are not cloudy all day." That is the kind of feeling we wish the whole world on Shabbos.

# CHAPTER 3

# TALKING TO GOD

O NCE, when I was a child, I saw my father with tears in his eyes. "Why are you crying, Papa?" I asked him. "Who hit you?"

"Nobody hit me," he replied. "I just talked to God."

"Oh," I said. "Does it hurt when you talk to God?"

"No, it doesn't hurt," he told me. "I'm just sad because I've waited so long."

That touched a chord very deep inside me. I remember sitting quietly with my mother when she would say the blessing over the Shabbos candles, making circular gestures in the air to bring the light into her heart, then covering her face with her hands. She would always pray for her family as well. As Mama got older she would include every one of her grandchildren and great-grandchildren in her prayer individually, and it took her a *while*.

This taught me what prayer is all about. Prayer is talking to

God. All my life, I have continued to seek out living models for how to connect to God from a deeper and more genuine place.

When I was sixteen, I chose to learn in the yeshiva of the Chabad, or Lubavitcher Hasidim. Their way really spoke to me. The idea of becoming a *lamdan,* a learned man, had no appeal to me: I wanted to find out more about how to connect with God. Every one of the Lubavitcher Rebbes had written something about how to *daven,* or pray. I learned so much from them.

I remember watching the head of our movement, Rebbe Yosef Yitzchak Schneersohn, the sixth Lubavitcher Rebbe, pray on the night of Rosh ha-Shanah. On Rosh ha-Shanah, Jews believe, God inscribes in a heavenly book the names of "who shall live and who shall die" in the coming year. On the fast of Yom Kippur, ten days later, the book of our fate is sealed. So Reb Yosef Yitzchak was not just chanting the prayers but pleading for his life and for the lives of his family, the community, and all creatures. This was 1942, a very hard year. In Europe the Holocaust was raging. Reb Yosef Yitzchak took about three hours to finish the *Amidah* prayer, weeping in front of the entire congregation. When you have a rebbe whose prayer is so strong, and you feel in your heart what a deep and genuine place his tears come from, your own prayer gets tuned to his. You learn how to talk to God.

From the Lubavitch, too, I learned that tears are not the only way to pray. One day in the yeshiva I was praying hard, swaying back and forth with my eyes shut tight and a grimace on my face as yeshiva boys do sometimes, almost as if I were trying to force God to listen to me, when suddenly I felt a *zetz* in the ribs and a whisper in my ear. *"Host du shoyn gepruft mit guten?"* Did you try asking nicely? Did you try already with a smile? It was Reb Yisroel Jacobson, our *mashpia,* or spiritual director, with whom we studied prayer and esoteric teachings twice daily. By the time I opened my eyes he had already continued down the aisle, but those six words had imparted an important lesson. Rabbi Nachman of Bratslav used to emphasize this. Perhaps our prayers are not answered, he suggested, because they don't have enough charm, enough grace. The Episcopal bishop Phillips Brooks agreed: Prayer is not overcoming God's reluctance, he said. It is taking hold of God's willingness. Our prayer should engage God as a lover would engage his beloved.

Now I am an old man, and I still find models for how to talk to God. Rabbi Shalom Noach Brazovsky, the Slonimer Rebbe, wrote a book called *Netivot Shalom* (Peaceful Ways) that spoke very simply and directly to the question of how we can become more acutely conscious and aware of what he believes is our inherent closeness to God. The Hasidic tradition placed great emphasis on this loving closeness or cleaving to God, which they call *devekut.* The Slonimer emphasizes that attaining devekut is not the problem: since we and all creation are constantly being re-created anew at every moment, as Hasidim believe, we are constantly in devekut. Our ears couldn't hear if they weren't in devekut. Our minds couldn't work if we weren't in devekut. Our hearts wouldn't beat it they weren't in devekut. The problem is only to be more *aware* that we are in devekut, to do everything we can to enhance that awareness. This kind of talk might seem strange to modern ears. It is not the way we usually look at the world. But to me this was such a different way of talking about our relationship with God. Instead of an intellectual struggle with all the logical implications of the act of prayer, here was a heart-centered, feeling way, one that was open to and inviting of experience.

His teachings touched me so deeply that when I was in Israel for my daughter's wedding, I asked a friend of mine to make an appointment with him. I was told that he was already an old man, that sometimes he's not quite sure what's going on, but I was so eager to meet him. Before going to see a rebbe, you immerse yourself in the *mikveh*. You go inside of yourself, trying to empty yourself out, to be a vessel to receive the Rebbe's blessing. I did these things before I was shown into his presence. "Rebbe," I said, "I come to ask you for a *gemilut chesed*"—a granting of a kindness.

"What's the *gemilut chesed* that you want?" he asked.

I said, "I just want you to recite the verse, '*Ve-yada'ata ha-yom*,' with your full awareness—just . . . just what you want us to understand from your book; and please hold my hand when you do that." I wanted to get the deepest, most direct transmission I could, on every level—mental, emotional, spiritual, and physical. The verse says, "Know this day and take to heart, that God is God everywhere, in the heavens above and the earth below: there is none other" (Deuteronomy 4:39). We recite it every day at the end of the *Alenu* prayer. This, Moses is saying, is the bottom line. This is the summary of awareness we should have.

The Slonimer looked up to his secretary and said in Yiddish, "*Nu, a Yid vos a farshtayt vos iz in meine sforim*, a Jew who understands what's in my books." He took my hand and held it to his chest and talked to me for twenty minutes. The sense of a transmission, the glimpse of the beautiful and exalted way in which a person like that can pray, was a profound experience. When you actually witness such a thing, it's like an invitation to a party of the spirit. The only question is whether you will answer it.

Have you ever been at a cafeteria and looked out the corner of your eye at the Christian family who fold their hands and make a blessing over the food? Such a simple gesture of piety is a beautiful thing to watch. That's why I always feel like a Peeping Tom when it comes to how people do it with God. When you're in a troublesome situation and you wish you could pray, it really helps to have been in the presence of people who *can* pray.

I believe that Jesus was modeling just such a connection in what became known as the "Our Father" prayer. Luke 11:1 tells us that "One of the disciples said to him, Lord, teach us to pray." The words that Jesus spoke then were all well-known at the time: they served as the simple, working person's prayer, a short version of prayer that encapsulates everything. "And he said to them, When you pray, say, Our Father who art in Heaven"—*avinu she-ba-shamayim;* "hallowed be thy name"—*yehei shmei raba mevorakh.* So what is Jesus saying? He is not prescribing the words. He is answering the question, "How shall we pray?" by demonstrating. The disciple said, "Teach us"; he said, "I'll *show* you." He's going into the experience himself, putting himself in a prayerful space, speaking words they all knew, but from his heart. Today only the words remain. But I believe he was trying to demonstrate that *what* you say is not as important as *how* you say it. What's important is placing ourselves in the presence of God and making a connection.

I learned a lot about ease and simplicity of prayer from Native Americans. When you hear Native Americans at prayer in the sweat lodge, you get a sense that we, for all the words in our prayer books, are illiterates at prayer. Their conversations with God seem so simple and direct. They're very relaxed about it. They take their time, and they really cover the waterfront. They say what's in their hearts and seem to have no sense of distance between themselves and God. That consciousness in the universe that can respond to their prayers is present and there. I remember going to a peyote meeting during the time that Nixon was president and listening to the local elder praying for the president. I thought, "Come on. For *Nixon* you pray?" But he said, "Dear God, this man at the White House, he may not know what he's doing, but he's got *such* a responsibility. So many people's lives are involved. Please guide him. Keep him happy. When he's unhappy and he feels bad, he makes bad things happen to people." And with each such request he would take a toke from his prayer cigar—tobacco rolled up in a corn leaf— and blow the smoke toward the peyote button so that his prayer should be accepted. Listening to him, I realized how hollow my prayer is if I don't address God in such a way, if I don't go into the vernacular from time to time with a real shopping list of things to take up with God.

Understanding the process of prayer, of talking to God, has been in a sense the major quest in my life. What really happens when we pray? What are the forces at work? How do the different elements of prayer affect us? How can we reshape the process of prayer so that it moves us as deeply today as it moved our ancestors in ancient times? We Jews have a fantastically rich tradition of talking to God. Our Torah contains over a dozen

Hebrew words and expressions for prayer. It is full of such conversations, from personal prayers of the heart to public prayers
on behalf of the entire people; from prophets and kings to shepherds, servants, and troubled parents; from praising and pleading
to arguing and even scolding. Our psalms and our *siddur,* or
prayer book, are treasure troves of letters to God. So talking to
God is not only a natural urge, it is a very Jewish one. How,
then, can we make this process more real for ourselves?

## START WHERE YOU ARE

To me, the act of prayer, though it seems so unnatural to the
modern mind, is in fact the most natural thing in the world. Our
desire to connect is so basic. We want to feel God's presence in
our lives. We want to offer our thanks. We want help and guidance. We need protection and encouragement. We may not feel
this urge every day, but sooner or later we will find ourselves
wanting or needing to pour our hearts out to that listening presence. Once we feel that presence in the universe, I believe that
some form of prayer will always happen naturally—if we let it.

The problem is that talking to God—far less asking God for
anything—has become hard for us. The very idea can wrap our
minds into a tangle of logical contradictions. What does it mean
to have a "God" who "listens" to my prayer? How could any
prayer of mine actually affect the outcome of anything—and if it
can't, what's the use of praying?

Moreover, we have learned to think of prayer as something

that happens in houses of worship, and what happens in our synagogues—the responsive readings, the cantor, the choir—rarely touches that feeling space inside us. The hushed reverence that synagogues try to preserve unfortunately inhibits any spontaneous expression of wonder or joy. I often imagine a mother taking her child to the synagogue for the first time. "We're going to go to the synagogue for Torah reading," she tells him. "And when the time comes, they will draw back the curtain and open up the doors of the ark, and in there is the Torah. And the Torah will be wearing a beautiful coat and a silver crown with tinkling bells! And then they'll take out the Torah and have a little parade, carrying the Torah around and singing, and everyone will kiss it. And then they will bring it up to the podium . . ."—she describes the whole process to the child. So they arrive at synagogue and the child keeps pulling at the mother. "When are they going to take out the Torah? Is it time for the Torah, Mommy? Is now the time?" And the mother says, "Not yet. . . . Not yet. . . . Not yet." Until finally the rabbi says, "All rise!" and the cantor sings out in a stentorian bellow, and then silence falls and the ark is opened. Then suddenly the child's delighted voice rings through the sanctuary: "Mommy, Mommy, look! The Torah, the Torah!"

And everybody turns around and goes, "SHHHHH!"

A person who comes to a house of worship is given a siddur. We open obediently to the proper page to see passages like, "O Heavenly King, vouchsafe us Your blessings." Our heads can't subscribe to this kind of language. We might notice that this disconnect applies to everybody else as well. "I bow down before thee," we read—but nobody's bowing. We read: "I will sing a new song and make a joyful noise unto the Lord," but just you try kicking up such a joyful racket and you'll quickly hear from the ushers. Storefront churches are full of worshippers clapping and jumping and yelling, "Halleluyah! Amen, brother! Tell it like it is!" but the words of our prayers have become unreal to us. Our eyes are reading one message, but our senses tell us something different. Our hearts are caught in the middle, confused and frustrated.

The prayers in our siddur were collected over centuries, but the siddur is not a museum vault of liturgical music and information. It is a living document. Like a coloring book, though, the siddur gives us only the outlines. Coloring those outlines in with life, context, feeling, is up to us. The siddur belongs not to the mind, but to the heart. If my wife tells me, "I love you," and I take that on the level of information, I would say, "Yes, dear, I know, you told me that yesterday." But of course she is not trying to tell me something I didn't know; she is trying to transmit a feeling. The same is true for the siddur. We're not trying to lay the same old praises at the feet of some old man in the sky; we're trying to connect with a being, a will, a love radiating out from the center of the universe—not the astrophysical center but the spiritual center—that can nourish something deep in our souls, something that has gotten very hungry among us.

Rather than reciting dutifully from the siddur, seek a genuine encounter. Take your time. Let the siddur speak for you. Daydream. Space out. Go where the images take you. A single phrase may be enough to transport you to a higher level. Make yourself transparent. Place yourself in the presence of God. This is what our siddur helps us to do.

. . .

A REAL CONVERSATION with God requires that we first of all start where we are.

A story is told of Rabbi Israel of Rizhin, the holy Rizhiner, great-grandson of the Maggid of Mezeritch, who was walking around the house of worship on the Ninth of Av, the fast day mourning the destruction of the Temple. He approaches one of the men who was rocking back and forth in misery like all the others and asks him, "Why are you crying?"

"Nu, Rebbe, it's the Ninth of Av. Why should I not cry?"

"But why are *you* crying?" the Rizhiner persists.

"Who, me? Why am *I* crying?"

"Yes, why are *you* crying?"

"Well, ah, Rebbe," the man stammers, "I—I am a *cohen,* a member of the priestly caste."

"So?"

"If the Temple had not been destroyed, Rebbe, I would get my meat for free, from the offerings."

"Stop crying," the Rizhiner tells him, "and I'll give you enough meat until next year."

"Yes, but, er, Rebbe, is it not written in the Talmud that the taste that used to be in the meat in the Temple days is now gone into the bone, so the meat doesn't taste as good?"

"You want bones?" the Rebbe says. "I'll buy you a whole heap of bones, enough for two years. So you can stop crying now."

"But Rebbe," the man says, "I don't have my teeth anymore. I couldn't get into those bones."

"Nu," says the Rizhiner, "then cry for your teeth—don't cry for the Temple!"

Don't talk to God about theory, the Rizhiner was saying. Tell God about your own personal loss. Start from your own immediate experience and offer that up to God. Prayer that does not come from the heart is no prayer at all.

Before we get fancy we need to make sure that our prayers are coming from a deep and honest place. Religious acts are—should be—no more than natural unfoldings of the human condition, of whatever situation we find ourselves in at any given moment. Our tradition, however, often starts from the other end, a top-down approach. Rather than working up from our own experience, it works down from our vision of a watchful and exacting Creator. Why did the Rabbis prescribe all the blessings that they did? "The earth is the Lord's and the fullness thereof," quotes the Talmud—but God has given the earth to us. The blessings are a means of restriking this bargain, of feeding some coins of the realm into the permissions machine. Theologically speaking, the Talmud's reasoning makes sense, but it does not speak to our hearts.

Whenever I talk about prayer, I always suggest not using the prayer book at first. Simply start where you are, whenever you feel inspired, and express the feelings that well up inside you. Use whatever name of God you are comfortable with.

"Dear God, thank you for this beautiful spring day."

"Oy, *Gottenyu,* thank you for my wonderful friends."

"Holy *Shekhinah,* eternal mother, I feel that my child is slipping away from me. Please help me know the best path to take."

"Master of the Universe, you know that I am ill. Please help me get through the day."

Or start with the traditional formula if you want. *"Barukh attah Adonai* (blessed are you, God) . . . thank you for this wonderful meal."

*"Barukh attah Adonai* . . . thank you for giving me dignified work. So many others are looking for employment, God. Please help them."

*"Barukh attah Adonai* . . . please help the world through these dark and dangerous times."

Expressing our feelings in this way helps us recover a sense of simplicity in talking to God.

Just as we can, at any time, spontaneously express the feelings that we want to convey to God, so can we put things in our own words whenever we are struck by a thought in the prayer book itself. Take the very first prayer in the morning, for example. The prayer reads: *"Modeh ani le-fanekha"* (I give thanks before thee, living and enduring King).

My own version might go something like this: "I know, God, that this being here is nothing but you in disguise. Thank you for wanting to play Zalman for another day. I'll do the best I can to give you a good ride. Please help me make this a noble day." Such thoughts give us a very genuine way of recalibrating ourselves for the day, of saying, not, "My will be done," but "Your will be done."

Even those of us who are comfortable with the liturgy can feel what we are saying more deeply if we take the time to put thoughts from the prayer book into our own words, in our native language. That's why I feel that using English is important. You may understand Hebrew, but unless you can think in that language, you won't feel it in the same way. I've seen so many students progress and start to go into the Hebrew more and more, only for the words to start becoming rote to them. Those who grew up with a Hebrew prayer practice have more of a problem with this than those who are approaching it fresh. The Hebrew is powerful and important, of course, but it shouldn't come at the price of losing the consciousness of what we are saying.

## BRINGING THE LITURGY TO LIFE

We have seen how expressing prayer in our own words helps us reconstitute the freeze-dried language in the siddur with the living water of our own experience. We can seek out other ways to help us make the leap of imagination that prayer challenges us to do. When I was on staff at Camp Ramah, the summer camp run by the Conservative movement, for example, I felt that a phrase like "who illuminates the earth and those who dwell upon her" didn't have any power at ten o'clock on a Shabbos morning, when we would usually recite it. So I used to get up before dawn and take the kids with me up to a mountain where we could watch the sun rise. Watching the sun come up in the east, hearing the animals begin their prayers—the birds beginning their song, the dogs barking in the valley below—was like a miracle. The experience of prayer welled up naturally in our hearts.

Tying a prayer to our own lived experience makes it so much more powerful. For example, the ArtScroll and some of the

older prayer books have a blessing to be recited upon seeing royalty: "Blessed art thou . . . who has given of his glory to flesh
and blood." One does not get to make this blessing very often.
But in Hasidism the metaphor of kingship is an important one:
the Jewish New Year, for instance, is seen as the time when we
crown the King anew. So I wanted to see a real coronation, to
be able to make the blessing and to mean it. When Queen Eliz-
abeth was crowned queen in June 1953, her coronation was
broadcast by live TV hookup—the transatlantic cable had just
been completed—and I stayed up to see how this young woman
was brought into the big cathedral at the Abbey church and
anointed with oil like the biblical kings. They sat her there and
handed her the scepter and the orb; and the Archbishop of Can-
terbury in his cope and miter, and the Lord Great Chamberlain
in his robes, and all these dignitaries bowed to her now that she
had been crowned. The awesome pomp and ceremony of this
investiture really gave me a sense of "who has given of his glory
to flesh and blood."

Simply by using our imaginations we can unpack the living
reality behind the words in amazing ways. This further deepens
and enhances even the most moving prayers. Take the Twenty-
third Psalm, for example.

*The Lord is my shepherd, I shall not want.*
*He maketh me to lie down in green pastures;*
*He leadeth me beside the still waters.*
*He restoreth my soul;*
*He leadeth me in the paths of righteousness, for His name's sake.*
*Yea, though I walk through the valley of the shadow of death,*

*I shall fear no evil, for Thou art with me;*
*Thy rod and Thy staff, they comfort me.*
*Thou preparest a table before me in the presence of mine enemies;*
*Thou anointest my head with oil, my cup runneth over.*
*Surely goodness and mercy shall follow me all the days of my life;*
*And I shall dwell in the house of the Lord forever.*

Who wrote this song? The first words are usually left out: "A song of David." So let's imagine the scene. Here is David. The prophet Samuel has already anointed him king, pouring oil on his head as was the custom. He can still feel it: "Thou anointest my head with oil." But Saul is still king, and David doesn't have too many friends outside his few devoted followers. His brothers aren't too happy: they are all older, but he, the runt in the family, is to be king. And King Saul is in a murderous rage at the man who will tear the kingship away from his house. Both Saul and the king of the Philistines are after David.

So David has a price on his head. He can't make a living yet, he doesn't have enough to eat, and he and his men are living like outlaws in a valley protected by rocky crags. Sometimes David ventures out, trying to bring some food back for them to eat. He has tried to knock on farmhouse doors, and people said, "Yea, what I have for you is that I'll tell King Saul where you're hiding." He barely manages to bring some food home in his bag, and he returns through the narrow ravines, through the windy little pass that leads into the hidden valley, the crags throwing their shadows on his path. Who might be waiting for him up there, arrows notched in their bows? He can't see who is above or behind him, and you can imagine the hair rising on the back of his neck, but finally he makes it. He tosses down his pouch with the food he's gotten. His men cook up some gruel on the fire, and he eats. Then he leans back with that telltale burp, and the men already know the look that comes over his face. "Quick," someone says, "the lyre." They pass him the lyre, and David starts plucking the strings. And there and then the psalm gets made.

He remembers his shepherd days, when things were easy and he wanted for nothing. He sees that there's no straight way to where he wants to go. That's what the Hebrew expression means: *ma'aglei tzedek* (circuitous paths of righteousness). He feels that God watches over him even when he walks those steep and dangerous paths of potential death.

When I need a crutch, Lord, he sings, I have thy rod and thy staff. The Hebrew contrasts the rod with which you get whipped and the crutch on which you lean. Both are of equal comfort to me, David says. Sometimes, when I deserve it, thy rod comes down swiftly—yes, God, thank you for reminding me. And when I need your staff to lean on, there it is. As for this food, Lord, I realize that if it were up to mine enemies, I wouldn't get any. And yet here we are, with enough to eat to live and fight on another day.

The song David sings is so full of his experience. The memory of gentler days, his present desperation, the sweating when he comes through the ravine: he sings about all this. Then he says, when I look at how life has been treating me up to now, surely goodness and mercy shall chase me all the rest of my days. I can relax in that faith; I don't have to be paranoid about it. It's like "I look over Jordan and what do I see? A band of angels coming after me."

In this way we can make the siddur our lyre, its lines the strings we pluck, searching for the words to express ourselves. Playing it sweetly takes practice—but it repays the effort, coming to our aid when our heart is troubled or angry or sad or overflowing with joy.

## A QUIET ORGASM OF THE SOUL

So far we have concentrated on our immediate experience of a prayer. We have seen how simply and naturally we can connect to God in our own words. We have seen how we can bring the words of prayer to life by imagining the reality behind them or tying them into our own experience. A third important way to experience prayer is to understand the different and successively deeper levels of ourselves that the siddur is designed to address; whereas at first glance the siddur may appear to contain just a long string of prayers, it is actually a program, perfected over many centuries, to help us create a rising curve of spiritual experience.

Nowhere can we see this curve more clearly than in the traditional morning prayers. Imagine a series of morning exercises whose purpose is not muscle tone but spiritual tone: a thought-rosary repeated every morning that readies us to meet the day as a person who lives in the presence of the divine. Creating that sequence is part of what the morning prayers are about. They are designed to build us up to a kind of peak, then to let us down gently so we can get on with our day. The morning prayers, a Hasidic saying tells us, are the Sabbath of the day, an island from which we set off on our forays into the everyday world.

The great Hasidic rabbi, Dov Baer of Lubavitch, taught that the first thought upon awakening has a lasting effect, setting the tone for the rest of the day. For traditional Jews this is the *Modeh Ani.* "I thank Thee, O ever-living and ever-existing King, for having returned my soul to me. Great is your faith in me." This act of thanksgiving and life affirmation is the daily eye-opener, calling us first to a devotional period instead of plunging us immediately into action. From there we proceed gradually with soul-stretching exercises before building up to more "heavy lifting," spiritually speaking—the higher goals of spiritual unification.

Building this kind of rising curve of spiritual feeling is not easy. At this level, following the sequence becomes important. That's why our prayer book is called the siddur, from the root *seder,* meaning order. Think of a well-planned meal. We don't dig right into the meat and potatoes. We might begin with something piquant to stimulate the appetite. Next we'd have a salad, to lay a base for what follows. Only then would we tuck into the main course. Then a glass of water to cleanse the palate, perhaps, before closing with something sweet to put a seal on our appetites. It flows if you get it in the right order. Good prayer, like good sex, good exercise, good learning, good conversation, needs to have a chance to build.

Many of our modern synagogues and churches don't achieve this. You hear a reading, you sing a hymn, you hear an announcement—it's nice, but emotionally flat. It doesn't take us anywhere. A good worship session should begin with awakening the body and the heart in what we might call "forepray," then rise and peak before it descends. Something close to a quiet orgasm of the soul has to happen. Otherwise, we'll walk away frustrated. So many of us are walking around with frustrated or frigid souls, souls that want to get to spiritual release but haven't had the opportunity to experience it.

The body of morning prayer is known as *Shacharit,* from the word *shachar,* or dawn. Shacharit takes us through four ever-higher levels. These stages of ascent reflect different sides of our-selves. We know God in different ways—just as we know everything else. The pragmatic side of us knows by doing. Our psychological side knows by feeling. Our philosophical side knows, you might say, by knowing. And our mystical side knows by intuiting. No single approach—pragmatic, psychological, philosophical, or mystical—would be enough to describe a whole person. We are all pragmatists when we go grocery shop-ping. We are feeling persons in love. Each of us is all of these things. And since we transmit and receive on all of these four frequencies, we need to give each aspect of ourselves a chance to reach out to God in its own way.


## WINDOW:
## AN OUTLINE OF DAILY PRAYERS

Jews have traditionally prayed three times a day, in addition to shorter prayers and blessings as the occasion demanded (blessings before and after food, before significant travel, etc.). The three daily prayers are *Shacharit* (morning), *Minchah* (afternoon), and *Ma'ariv* (evening or night), of which Shacharit is by far the longest. All these can be found in any prayer book. The following is an out-line of the morning prayers, including the names of the best-known prayers in each section:

- Preliminary prayers like *Modeh Ani,* blessings for washing hands, putting on tzitzit, etc.
- The morning blessings or *Birkot ha-Shachar,* including *Mah Tovu,* the blessings for tallis and tefillin, *Adon Olam, Yigdal,* and a series of blessings designed to parallel the process of waking up and joining the world.
- The "tuneful verses," or *Pesukei de-Zimra,* including A*shrei,* five "Hallelujah!" psalms, and the Song of the Sea (Exodus 15:1–18).
- The *Shema* with the paragraphs that precede and follow it.
- The nineteen-blessing silent devotion, or *Amidah.*

The silent devotion is the peak of all three daily services. What follows represents a gradual descent and afterthoughts.

- When praying in a quorum, or minyan, the cantor repeats the *Amidah* aloud.
- The *Tachanun,* or supplications, for forgiveness.
- When praying in a minyan, the Torah is read aloud on Mondays and Thursdays.
- Concluding prayers, including *Ein ke-Elohenu* and *Alenu.*

The afternoon and evening prayers include greatly shortened ver-sions of Shacharit. Sabbath and festival prayers follow the same basic pattern, with changes and additions, but traditionally include the *Musaf,* or added prayer, after Shacharit on the Sabbath and holidays, and a fifth prayer, the *Ne'ilah,* or concluding service, recited on Yom Kippur only. The Musaf and Ne'ilah service, like the other three, both build up to their own *Amidah.*

## Doing: The Morning Blessings

At the first level of morning prayers we find the *Birkot ha-Shachar,* or "dawn blessings." These are directed at the level of physical experience. Blessed are you, God, we say, for helping us to distinguish between night and day; for giving us the power to see; for clothing us; for making us free and helping us stand tall; for helping us walk with certainty, providing our needs, and giving us strength.

I usually accompany the morning blessings with some body movement. The mouth is a serial instrument: I can only say one thing at a time. But on a physical level I experience and express many things simultaneously. Imagine all your organs contributing to the performance: your heart beating out the rhythm, your lungs playing the wind instruments, your vocal cords the strings, your limbs dancing, your brain conducting. If I want my total self to know God, I want to bring that physicality into action as much as I can.

Early in the morning prayers, we recite a series of blessings designed to parallel the movements of a waking person: becoming conscious, opening the eyes, stretching, straightening up, stepping on the floor, putting on clothes and belt and head covering. I always try to give these some physical dimension. Each person would do this differently, of course. The following is just an example of the kind of holy yoga we can do in the morning.

We say, "Blessed are you, Yah, who gives the heart understanding to distinguish between day and night." I listen for sounds of my neighborhood waking up: people, dogs, birds, whatever I can hear.

"Blessed are you, Yah, for making me in Your image." I think of the human body, created in the shape of YHVH, the name of God. I think of my head as the *yud,* the first letter in God's name; my shoulder and arms as the *heh;* my spine as the *vav;* and my pelvis and legs as the other *heh.*

"Blessed are you, Yah, who gives sight to the blind." I open my eyes and feel the miracle that I should be able to see!

"Blessed are you, Yah, who clothes the naked." I say this as I am putting on my clothes.

"Blessed are you, Yah, who releases the imprisoned." I strrrrrrretch my arms wide as a sign of freedom.

"Blessed are you, Yah, who straightens the bent." I bow down with every vertebra of my spine before straightening up.

"Blessed are you, Yah, who spreads the earth upon the waters." I rock back and forth on my heels and toes, grateful that I'm standing on firm ground.

"Blessed are you, Yah, who firms a person's steps." I step back, trusting I will fall into no abyss.

"Blessed are you, Yah, who has provided me with every need." I make a circular motion with my arms to symbolize a

cornucopia waiting for me, remembering how many times in my
life I was provided for.

"Blessed are you, Yah, who girds Israel with strength." The
last word here is *gevurah,* the divine attribute of strength. I bellow out the last syllable— *"ge-vu-RAH!"*—letting my voice express the strength I feel inside.

"Blessed are you, Yah, who crowns Israel with splendor." Before you go out in the morning you look in the mirror. Am I
dressed? Is my halo on the right way? You don't want to go with
a kvetchy face, so you get your thoughts in order and smile.
That's what this blessing means to me at this time of day.

Finally I squeeze all my muscles together, tight, tight, tight,
until I have no more strength left, and then I relax and feel the
energy start flowing into me, and I make the last blessing:
"Blessed are you, Yah, who gives strength to the weary."

## DOORWAY:
## FILLED WITH YOUR GLORY

The morning blessings are not the only parts of the davening we
can express physically. Once I was working with a group of high
school kids who were so full of pepper they couldn't sit still.
When we got to the cantor's *Amidah* repetition, I suggested that
we recite the responsive verse that goes "Holy, holy, holy, the
Lord of Hosts, the whole earth is filled with your glory" like this.
Try it with a group of friends if you can.

"Let's close our eyes," I told them, "and for the first 'holy' let's hold our hands, palms together, over our hearts, and summon that feeling we have when we come into a sacred space.

"For the second 'holy,' let's take our hands up to our heads, and think, 'Oy, "holy." What do I understand about holiness and sacredness?'

"For the third 'holy,' let's raise our arms up over our heads, as high as we can, as if to say, 'If holy is only what I understand it to be, it wouldn't be holy enough! It's beyond that.'

"Then, as we say 'Lord of hosts,' let's gather our hands together on our hearts, interpreting 'hosts' not as armies, which is the original Hebrew meaning, but using the English sense of the word: 'I am the host inviting God to dwell within me.'

"Finally, as we say, 'The whole world is filled with your glory,' let's sweeeeep our arms around in a half circle and open our eyes and look around, making eye contact with our friends and seeing the beauty all around us. 'The whole world is filled with your glory!'"

And so for five minutes the place was transformed, all of us moving our arms and turning and chanting, giving a channel to all the energy they had: not asking it to change, but using it to make a connection.

## Feeling: The Songs of Praise

The second section contains the *Pesukei de-Zimra,* or "tuneful verses." This section corresponds to the world of emotions, of feelings, of celebration. Most famous of these songs of praise is the *Ashrei* prayer, which is followed by five psalms that begin and end with the same word: Halleluyah! Here we are not yet asking for anything; we are simply praising God. I sing "Halleluyah!" because I can't help it, almost like Peter Pan in the musical, who crows like a rooster because "I gotta crow!"

Whereas the morning blessings emphasize the physical, songs and wordless tunes, or *nigguns,* are very important in connecting *emotionally* to God. Singing conveys the feeling content of a prayer in a way that mere words cannot. "Halleluyah! Sing to the Lord a new song," one of the psalms begins. Sometimes I go to a little keyboard I have near my davening space and improvise a new niggun or tune. If only I could remember all the niggunim I made up! But to make this real for myself I want to "sing to the Lord a new song" every time. This is a wonderful section in which to focus on a particular sentence or phrase that speaks to us. Taking a love song that you know and sending it out to God can work beautifully as well.

You don't have to be an expert in prayer or in music to sing to God. All it takes is intention. I was once at the Lama Foundation, a spiritual center in New Mexico, on Father's Day. I said to them, let's sing to God, "Happy Father's Day to You." So we sang it, and everybody was laughing and giggling. It sounded so silly at first! Then I said to them, "Let's do it again. And you remember you can go from the sublime to the ridiculous? Let's go from the ridiculous to the sublime." And so we did, singing several rounds of "Happy Father's Day to You" with wonderful intention and sweetness.

Singing in a group brings hearts together in a way that might not happen otherwise. Some years ago I was invited by the young leadership of the United Jewish Appeal to lead the Friday night service at a huge gathering in New York. What a scene! Elie Wiesel was speaking later on that night. Upstairs the John Birch Society was having a meeting in the same hotel. Downstairs we were an enormous conglomeration of Jews from many denominations and communities, with barely enough prayer books to go around. The PA system was barely adequate; the air-conditioning was broken, and fans were blowing all over the place. Noise? *Meshuggeh.* I come down with my Hasidic garb, which I wore in those days, to find twelve rabbis sitting there in the middle of the room, leaning back, arms folded, skeptical looks on their faces: "We want to see how this guy's going to handle this." After sizing up the situation I walked over to the rabbis and said, "*Chaverim, rabbonim,* friends and teachers. You realize this is an impossible service, right? So I'm going to try to do this with Stephen Foster melodies because that's the only thing that I can count on everybody knowing. I *beg* of you to disperse yourselves among the crowd and not sit in one group. And please help me out and sing out loud, because I'll be embarrassed if you don't." And they did! We sang *"Lekha Dodi"* (Come, my friend, to greet the Bride) to the tune of "Beautiful Dreamer." We sang the *Hashkivenu* prayer to "Autumn Leaves":

*O Grant that we*
*lie down in peace*
*secure in thy*
*protecting love . . .*

We finished with *Adon Olam* to the tune of "Shenandoah." It was a wonderful service, and everybody went along with it. True, your average synagogue might not have allowed something like this. But this was an emergency situation: I couldn't think of any other way to unite this huge and disparate gathering in an act of true worship. But these wonderful American tunes, so deeply rooted in all of us, were able to bring us all together, to carry us there, so to speak.

## Knowing: The Shema

At the third level of the morning prayers we find the *Shema* with the blessings that precede and follow it. This part takes us into the philosopher's way. It invites us to reflect on the nature of reality in the universe. The language here envisions God's praise on a galactic scale. "Who forms light and creates darkness . . . who illuminates the earth and those who dwell there . . . whose ministering angels stand at the summit of the universe." We have all seen pictures of angels, little guys in nightshirts with wings flying around. We're not talking about that here; we're talking about the universe! At this point our prayer landscape fills with gigantic heavenly beings from the visions of Isaiah and Ezekiel, creatures with barely translatable names, *serafim* and *ofanim* and the holy *chayot*. Even such an authority as Maimonides admits that we know very little about these beings, but the imagery is clearly meant to stretch our minds to the limit. I think of the gallery of photographs at the Hubble Telescope's Web site. I remember that *ofanim* comes from the word *ofan,* or wheel: these,

to me, are the planets. I imagine the *chayot ha-kodesh,* or holy
creatures, as the zodiac constellations. I think of the burning *serafim* as the galaxies. I imagine vast galaxy clusters saying "HOLY,
HOLY, HOLY," and others answering with thunderous noise,
"BLESSED IS GOD'S GLORY." I think of a universe radiating
consciousness, being, bliss, ecstasy, life, death. I think of the dance
that scales down that energy until it comes to cells, atoms, and
quarks. You can see how even a few minutes of such an exercise
can open up our minds in the morning.

This is the language that takes us into the *Shema.* "Hear,
O Israel, YHVH our God, YHVH is One." Listen, hear, and
understand—you, me, and every one of us: God, on all levels of
reality, is ECHAD.

One.

Unique.

Infinite.

All encompassing.

This *echad* is beyond our ability to grasp. At this point the
mind declares bankruptcy. In the moment of unity we have nothing to hold on to. We are lost in God, but being still in our bodies at the same time, our reason sets off an alarm and says, "No!
It's not true!" Here intellect must surrender to intuition, for intuition can bear paradox and leap, if only for a split second, to
true identity with God.

The following verse brings us back to the world: *"Barukh shem
kevod malkhuto . . ."* I translate this as, "Through time and space
your glory shines, Majestic One." Here at least I can imagine the
dimensions of space and time filled by that miraculous *something.*

The *Shema* addresses not only the mind: we say, "Let these words which I command you this day be upon your heart." One of our teachers, Reb Mendele Kotzker, asks: Why *upon* the heart? Because only in rare moments does our heart truly open up. But if we carry these thoughts on top of our heart, then when the heart opens for a moment they are ready to drop into it and take root.

## Intuiting: The *Amidah*

Finally we reach the highest point in the davening, the silent *Amidah*. This is, on the one hand, the most exalted place of all, the highest Kabbalistic level, the place we can only know by intuition, by a process that completely circumvents our cognitive faculties. Silence is an important part of our attempt to approach such a place. Aryeh Kaplan, a wonderful Kabbalist who died young, observed in one of his books, *Kabbalah and the Bible,* that there are some five hundred words in the morning *Amidah*. If you devoted an entire hour to saying the *Amidah,* you would say one word every seven seconds. Can you imagine what it feels like to daven that way? Next time you're in synagogue or want to pray by yourself, try it with a phrase you find that inspires you. Don't stretch the words. Keep them short and let the space around them fill with meaning.

On the other hand, just as I am standing in silence at that highest place, an "Ouch" comes up, a need. "Dear God, I have *no* idea what I need to do. I feel so out of phase with you. Please help me." Like a child with a compassionate parent, I find that all my concerns start coming to the surface. I always encourage people who are saying the *Amidah* to express their own thoughts in any of the nineteen blessings. For example:

The prayer reads: "*Hashiveinu avinu le-toratekha,* bring us back to your Torah."

We might add: "Dear God, I feel I'm not in harmony with your will. Please take over. I don't want any other will but your will for me at this point."

The prayer reads: "*Selach lanu avinu ki chatanu,* forgive us, Father, for we have sinned."

We might add: "Master of the Universe, I know that some of the things that I've done were wrong. I'm feeling ashamed. I don't know if I can fix them myself. If there's anything that I need to fix myself, please enlighten me. Show me how I can make it up to those I have harmed. And if, God forbid, I can't do anything about it, then please forgive me and wipe this away. I don't want this sitting in my craw all the time."

The prayer reads: "*Hashiva shofteinu ke-va-rishonah,* restore our judges as of old."

We might add: "Oy, God, I'm worried about the state of justice in our country. We are not treating rich and poor alike, as Torah told us to do. Please guide the president to appoint fair judges, and help all of us to judge our fellow beings with compassion."

The prayer reads: "*Modim anachnu lakh,* we thank you."

We might say: "*Gottenyu,* it feels so good to give thanks to you. I thank you for the thanksgiving!"

The prayer reads: "*Elohai netzor leshoni mei-ra,* God, guard my tongue from evil."

We might say: "Dear God, I just don't want to forget myself and what I'm all about. Please help me stay on track, and help me not to say anything that would harm anybody in any way."

Before I had my Palm Pilot, I used to carry in my pocket a 3 x 5 card that I'd laminated with tape so I could write on it and erase it to my heart's content. I had a list of what every section of the *Amidah* was about: consciousness, repentance, forgiveness, strength to overcome difficulties, and so on. And whenever something came up that I wanted to take up with God, I'd take out the card and write it down.

This same process can take us all the way through to the final *Alenu,* as we pause before chanting that well-known tune to express our own feelings on the subject:

The prayer reads: "*Alenu le-shabe'ach la-adon ha-kol,* it is our duty to praise the Master of all."

We might say: "Master of the Universe, now that I've finished praying I know that I haven't even started! But that's all I can do for today. I want you to know that *alenu le-shabe'ach,* and so on."

The Torah does not prescribe a liturgy for prayer. The prayers in the siddur were established by the Rabbis, and in saying them we fulfill a rabbinical mitzvah. And yet Torah tells us, "When you are troubled, you shall find the words" (Deuteronomy 4:30).

Rebbe Shalom Dov Baer of Lubavitch teaches in his *Kuntres ha-Tefillah* (Treatise on Prayer) that when we turn to God with what is truly in our hearts—when we are able to fill the prayers in the siddur with so much meaning as to make them our own—then we transcend the rabbinic injunction to pray and fulfill a commandment from Torah itself. This is what we are trying to do here.

## WINDOW:
## THE FOUR WORLDS SIDDUR

The four-tier approach to prayer was first elaborated by the Holy Ari of Safed, Isaac Luria (1534–1572) and the Kabbalists who surrounded him. These Kabbalists imbued every word of the davening with mystical intention. To them, every word of prayer had the potential to turn us into a purer receptacle of divine light and to hasten the time of redemption.

They saw the morning davening as an ascent through four successively higher worlds that lead toward the *En-Sof,* or Infinite. The dawn prayers represent the world we see around us, the world of physical *asiyah,* or action. The verses of attunement represent the world of *yetzirah,* or formation, the level of feelings and emotions. The *Shema* and the blessings around it represent the world of *b'riah,* or creation, while the silent *Amidah* represents the very highest world of *atzilut* or pure emanation. The gentle descent of the prayers after the *Amidah* were included in this model as well. Kabbalists referred to the confession that follows the *Amidah* as the "vestiges of *atzilut,*" while the final prayers that followed, including the *Alenu,* were called the "descent of nourishment," helping us to bring back to our daily lives the healing and blessings and insight that we picked up in the higher worlds. The Kabbalists believed that one could hope to effect such an ascent only through the most intense *kavanah,* focus or devotion. They thus devised and added to the siddur a whole series of *kavanot,* prayers of intention, to help worshippers focus their thoughts toward specific names of God.

In the centuries following Luria's death, the teachings and liturgical innovations of the Ari and his contemporaries were adopted throughout the Jewish world. Even the ancient Bene Israel congregation in Bombay once used the *nusach* or version of the Ari, as I learned on a visit there in 1982. The Ari's innovations are not common knowledge to us today because they were suppressed during the rationalist Enlightenment, which rejected all this talk of mystical attainment and attunement. But the symphonic poesy of consciousness that the Ari's nusach represented is acutely relevant to our psychological and spiritual search.

## PRAYING IN COMMUNITY

The synagogue—our spiritual home since the Temple was destroyed—has changed over the centuries. For the last hundred and fifty years, especially, the Ashkenazic or North European communities and their American descendants have been dominated by what the Greeks used to call the Apollonian approach, seeking a faith that was rational, well-ordered, in tune with what the sciences tell us about the world. But so thorough has the rationalist influence become that we need to be reminded that our long history contains another approach as well: one the Greeks used to call Dionysian (after Dionysius, the god of wine), which is fancy language for direct, intuitive, loving, charismatic, ecstatic.

In some respects, the nineteenth century did a good job: Enlightenment thinking, for example, demanded the translation of prayers into languages that worshippers could understand. But the rationalists threw a lot of baby out with the bathwater. The more forward-looking Jews who came to America were bent on fitting in with modern society. They wanted services in English, organs in the synagogues, and the liturgy stripped of anything that did not jibe with a modern viewpoint. We tapped rabbis for their minds, their eloquence, their ability to give sermons and to govern congregations—but not necessarily for their deep spirituality. This bias in turn shapes the synagogues we build, the services we hold, and the congregations that attend them.

The most fun I ever had in shul as a child in Vienna was on Simchat Torah, the holiday that celebrates the completion of our year-long reading of the Torah, when we kids would get to parade around the podium in shul holding a flag with an apple or candle on top. Then we would stand aside and the Hasidim would begin to dance, and sometimes Pop or someone else would lift me onto their shoulders and dance with me. We would dance and sing on Purim and other festivals, too, and at weddings. But when an orderly, rationalist approach placed fixed pews in synagogues, we could no longer push the chairs and benches aside and begin a dance. Those whose hearts yearned to express the celebrative, ecstatic part of themselves—who wanted to get up and *dance,* or sing and clap their hands—too often turned elsewhere or stayed home. No wonder more than half the Jewish people is missing from our congregations!

So when you go synagogue-shopping, see how good the congregation is at bringing the freeze-dried liturgy alive. Take a look what they do in the middle of the week. See what classes they're offering: how they involve the kids, the parents, the elders. Look at the library. Watch how the rabbi does a bar mitzvah, if that's what you need to do. You're making an investment! Soul maintenance deserves money and time, and it deserves doing it properly.

Of course, we as individuals need to get involved as well. I don't mean to join a committee; I mean getting our hearts and souls involved. Judaism has become a consumer industry. Attending synagogue can be like boarding an airplane: "Put on your seat belt, we'll take you for a ride, give you a nice landing, then you can get off. Thank you for flying Emanuel." What we want is more producer Judaism, where we're coproducers of our Jewish life along with the rabbi and cantor.

If you're a member of a shul and you have spiritual needs, tell your rabbi about them. A rabbi should be able to pray with you and for you when you have trouble, but our rabbinical seminaries are not training our rabbis to do this. Imagine somebody comes for a pastoral appointment. They start telling him their *tzores,* and the rabbi, before giving them any answer, says gently, "Come, let's pray about this." What a difference that would make. It's not a common response, but you can help the rabbi with this by communicating your needs and perhaps even leading the way.

If the service is not fulfilling your spiritual needs, you can communicate this as well. "Listen, Rabbi, I have this need, and I think other people do, too. I feel spiritually starved, but I don't have an outlet for this in our shul, so please help me with this." It's astonishing how few shuls make time in the service for us to express our spiritual concerns. When the ark is opened, for example, we tell the congregation to rise and everybody sings along respectfully. In many congregations we still sing the old Aramaic words, "*ve-tashlim mish'alin de-liba'i*," asking God to "fulfill the wishes of my heart." But we don't take the time to focus on what our hearts truly want. Perhaps it would be better—and some congregations have begun to do this—if instead the rabbi said, "Please be seated. Now that the ark is open, we will have a quiet period, so that anyone who wishes to may pray about the things that most concern them." This would allow us some time to really communicate: "Oy, God, now that the ark is open I feel a little closer. I need to tell you, I'm concerned about my job, concerned for my ability to provide for myself and my family. Here I was hoping I had a decent retirement nest egg and now the dot-coms have killed it for me. I'm *worried.*"

Of course, praying in community is not easy. We all have our opinions about the rabbi and the others in the congregation. Even if we're one of the people who attends regularly, we can still feel that we're spinning our wheels; that we're not *going* anywhere, spiritually speaking. We don't have high expectations that anything will happen in our worship together, that we will achieve any breakthroughs. That is why it can be helpful, when you first enter the synagogue and sit down, to take a few minutes to get your bearings as a member of the congregation before you open your siddur. Look at the people around you with the spirit of generosity in your heart. Remember the famous phrase *"ve-ahavta le-re'acha kamocha,"* love thy neighbor as thyself. The people sitting here, they all have their *tzores,* their *gesheften,* the problems that crop up in their lives; they're working hard, trying to pay their mortgage, to lead a decent life. Try to look at each one with compassion and call down a *b'rakhah* for each one. Do the same for the rabbi and the people who help run the services. Looking around at your fellow worshippers with compassion and forgiveness and love; tuning in to the purpose that brings you all together under one roof, no matter how haltingly it's expressed, will begin to give you a real sense of another important verse that leads off our prayers in the morning: *"Mah tovu ohalekha Ya'akov*: How good are thy tents, O Jacob; thy dwelling places, Israel."

A gathering for the purposes of prayer is holiness in potential. The Rabbis had a saying: whenever ten gather, the holy presence dwells in their midst. I don't think this means merely a gathering of ten bodies. If disagreements well up within the gathering and the sense of community has been injured, then oy, the *Shekhinah,* the holy presence, is not there. But when healing takes place, and we are present as one, then the *Shekhinah* becomes present. The only way to get it together—is together. When together we create a sense of "Come, all ye faithful," or as we sing on Friday night, "Come, let us sing to the Lord," something happens in the room that is very palpable. You can actually feel the presence of the *Shekhinah.*

Find as many ways as you can to be present *actively.* When the service calls for an "Amen" or other response, speak right up. "Amen" has become so ceremonialized that we often forget the meaning of the word: "That's the truth! Right on! Tell it like it is!" If singing is called for, sing out. Clap your hands if you feel moved to do so: more often than not you'll find that other daveners have only been waiting for permission to do the same. If you can add a line of harmony, go right ahead. If nobody's dancing in the aisle, move your hips and shoulders in your seat. Do whatever you can to send the prayers *up*, to lift the energy level.

If, on the other hand, you are participating in the service, and you get to a line that speaks to you, stay with it. Say you come to a line like, "If our feet would be as swift as hinds; if we had wings like eagles." Suddenly you space out. If I had wings like that, oy, would I soar! I wouldn't have to push very hard, I'd just move those little feathers at the very end—like Jonathan Livingston Seagull . . . soaring . . . almost motionless—you know? A minute ago you were merely reading, but suddenly you're free. You're flying with your davening! So feel free to space out in this way, and if you can, find a person with whom you can share such things after the prayers are over.

Never allow yourself to be bored. Take a good book to shul, something that is inspirational for you. If you want, wrap it so that people won't see the cover. If you're bored with the service, and you read, let's say, a story from Buber's *Tales of the Hasidim,* you can find a way to retune yourself to the purpose in the room.

Even when we're just sitting and listening to a sermon, we can become active listeners. Next time the rabbi is preparing to begin the sermon, ask yourself: "What would I like to hear from God today?" And keep beaming your question at the rabbi. I believe that God uses these instruments, and that you will often get help with your question without the rabbi's even being aware of it. I can't tell you how many times people have said to me, "Do you remember what you said to me years ago?" More often than not I don't remember. But I believe that the reason a message got through was because they were coming to me in an open and questing mode. A question is like a container waiting to be filled. If we come empty-handed, we have nothing in which to carry away answers, but if we come with our containers, chances are we will find contents to fill them.

## FOR THE LOVE OF GOD

Prayer is known as *avodah she-ba-lev,* the service of the heart. The mitzvah of prayer, whether we approach it individually or as a group, is the most pleasant duty of all: a duty of love. In offering up the contents of our hearts in prayer, we fulfill the mitzvah that opens the very first paragraph of the *Shema:* Love God. The idea of loving God may sound abstract, but it is not: the love of God is simply a more transcendent form of the love that we feel in our hearts for those around us every day.

The Kabbalist Reb Eliyahu de Vidas relates the following tale in the name of Reb Isaac of Acre: Once there was a man, a simple person, who was walking in the forest by a river, and there, by the river in the forest, he saw a princess bathing and fell in love with her. In the coming days he couldn't eat, he couldn't sleep: such longing and yearning for her came over him that he didn't know what to do. He went to the gates of the palace and waited there for days and days until finally, one day, the princess went out riding. As she passed him, he jumped up on her carriage and held on to the door and told her how much he loved her, and how much he wanted to be with her. Was there any way they could possibly be together? he asked. "Oh, sure," she answered. "In the cemetery."

Of course she meant it as a dismissal, but he takes her at her word. He goes straight to the cemetery and sits down to wait for her, and every day he says, "She'll meet me here in the cemetery, I know she will. She'll keep her word. And I will wait for her until she does, as long as it takes." Every day he runs quickly into town and begs a little bit so he'll have something to eat, then goes right back to the cemetery and sits down again to think about his princess and how beautiful she is. She is so firmly fixed in his heart and his mind that he can just focus on her and immediately her face appears before him with radiant clarity.

As the days pass and he goes deeper and deeper into contemplating her beauty, he begins to ask: What is the beauty behind this beauty? What gives this charm such charm? And he begins to penetrate from physical beauty to metaphysical beauty. Gradually, after years of such meditation, he becomes a very holy person. People come to the cemetery and they see that his face is transformed. They come to him for advice, and they come to him for blessings, and word starts to spread that a *tzaddik* lives out there in the cemetery, a righteous and holy man who can bestow wonderful blessings.

Meanwhile, the princess has married, but years have passed and she hasn't had any children. One day, a lady-in-waiting tells her of this holy man in the cemetery who gives blessings to everybody. Why doesn't she go and get herself a blessing? So she comes to the cemetery to ask for a blessing. She doesn't recognize him, but he recognizes her, and after giving her his blessing, thanks her for serving as the vessel that moved him to contemplate the ever-deeper layers of beauty in the world until he came to God.

Reb Eliyahu adds a postscript: Anybody who wants to approach God and the love of God, he says, and hasn't loved another human being with all their hearts, what do they know? Through manifesting the love that's in our hearts and seeking its ultimate source, the story tells us, we find a path to holiness. Judaism works best, I believe, for those who seek to fulfill what Bahya ibn Pakuda, in the title of his famous book, called *Chovot ha-L'vavot,* the duties of the heart. When we can perform the duties of the heart, then all the rest of it works. What are those duties? Acts of conscience. Acts of faith. Acts of purification. Acts of repentance and return to our source. Acts of attunement to that presence we have felt in the universe.

Prayer—the opportunity to talk to God—can help us learn this, if only we approach it with heart. If the Baal Shem Tov taught us anything, it is that the heartfelt prayers of an unlearned person are worth more than all the perfunctory prayers of scholars. When we approach God, it is best to turn off our mental computers and tune in to our feelings, even if this makes us self-conscious or foolish in our own eyes. Once we open up our hearts, we will find an infinite number of things to confide to that presence, because God godself is infinite. Once we open up our hearts, we will find ourselves plunged into a love story like the tzaddik in the cemetery, contemplating Her infinite loveliness and struggling—despite all the numerous prayers in our prayer book—to answer the question: "Where do I begin?"

# CHAPTER 4

# THE MEANING OF MITZVAH

TODAY we are all Jews by choice. Usually we say this of those who undertake the great transformative journey of converting. But if we look a little bit deeper, in an open society we are all Jews by choice. We no longer live in the shtetl, where everyone knew how often we went to synagogue and the pressure to conform to a certain level of piety was enormous. We no longer subscribe to the classic model of divine reward and punishment. Nobody is looking over our shoulders: we are completely free to decide whether and to what extent we want to make Judaism a part of our lives.

On the other hand, this freedom puts the ball in our court. No one—no rabbi, no therapist, no guru—can take responsibility for our spiritual lives. We have to do that ourselves. If I want to feel a spiritual presence in my life, I can't wait until all the evidence is in about whether God exists or not. I have to begin

with an affirmation—a declaration, as it were, of what's important to me. I have to make a leap. The promise of Judaism or any
spiritual system is that if we make that leap, things will begin to
open up for us. Transformation will start to happen.

The leap that Judaism asks us to make is not a leap of faith,
but a leap of action. *Ta'amu u-re'u,* as Psalms 34:9 tells us: Taste
and see. This will only become a reality if you dare to get your feet
wet. Do you hunger for spirituality? Take on some form of spiritual practice and you will begin to satisfy that hunger. Start as
small as you want. Our tradition has a saying: perform one holy
deed, and another will quickly come in its wake.

THE JEWISH VISION of spirituality in action is based on *mitzvot*
(singular: *mitzvah*), a word usually translated as commandments,
from the root *tz-v-h,* commanded. But in a world without kings,
in a democratic society, the word *commandment* has lost its power.
The old understanding of being commanded was of commandments handed down on the mountain, of an authority beaming
down upon us from above. Today any sense of commandment
must come from within, from inside us.

Can we feel commanded without feeling coerced? That is a
central question for us today. Can we become party to this holy
relationship, one that calls us to our ideal, to be the best that we
can be? Can we take on that sense of intention and responsibility?
Understanding what Judaism means by a mitzvah will help us answer this question, for the word's resonance and nuance extend far
beyond a quick definition like "commandment" or "good deed."

A mitzvah, in the traditional sense, is any act Jews believe to be required of us by God. It is a prayerful or worshipful action. Some mitzvot are simply good common sense, like keeping our surroundings clean or not putting ourselves in danger. But performing that action consciously, as a mitzvah, draws us into a higher level of dialogue with the universe. In doing a mitzvah we act not only from whim, or because it is in our interest to do so, or because this act seems logical at the time, but with a higher sense of intentionality. We act out of a desire to communicate with that holy presence we have felt. Touching a mezuzah as I go through a doorway is a way of connecting, of saying to that presence, "Hello, God, it's me."

As our practice deepens, our relationship grows more intimate. A mitzvah feels like a glance exchanged between lovers across a crowded room. The blessing that accompanies many mitzvot thanks the God "who sanctified us with his commandments." The word for "sanctified" (kid'shanu) derives from the word kaddosh, holy. Kaddosh is also at the root of the word for "consecrated" (mekuddeshet), which we say as part of a traditional Jewish wedding: "By this you are consecrated to me." As the wedding ring consecrates one partner to the other, so each mitzvah we do consecrates us to God. The blessing turns each new mitzvah into another wedding ring, as it were, that seals this holy relationship. Unlike a wedding, though, this reaffirmation happens every day. When my wife and I perform the ritual washing of hands before eating bread, we take off our rings, as traditional Jews sometimes do, so the water will touch every part of our hands. Then Eve puts my ring back on my finger, and I put her

ring back on hers. Similarly, the mitzvot remind us daily—
hourly—of our commitment to the holy.

Most mitzvot have both physical and mental components.
The physical component, of course, lies in actually performing the
mitzvah, which may be doing a desirable act or refraining from
an undesirable one. Performing a mitzvah for the first time can
affect us in different ways. Sometimes our experience is: "I lit
candles last Friday night, but it's not working. I didn't feel anything." Other times we bring our highest intentions and pent-
up yearning to that first time and feel a tremendous rush of
consciousness and awareness—but have a hard time recapturing
that peak the second, third, or fourth time around.

The rabbis realized this. Rabbi Elimelekh of Lizhensk says,
"If you want to start something new, do it for forty days to get
it going." Steadiness is important. Every time we perform the
mitzvah we get more deeply involved, more deeply entrained—
even if that change is happening imperceptibly, below our conscious radar. The preliminary practices of Vajrayana Buddhism call
for 100,000 prostrations. We might ask, "If a hundred thousand
prostrations will work, then surely I should feel something by
the tenth prostration?" But it doesn't work that way. Our heads
are still much too engaged, our egos too defended. The repeti-
tive aspect of ritual, doing something again and again, sooner or
later manages to sneak around our intellectual defenses—but
only if we keep doing it long enough to drop our mental stop-
watch and checklist, to stop asking, in effect, "Are we there yet?"
Repetition does things to the mind. It is often the only way to
experience a mitzvah's beauty and power. But we have no short-
cut to that effect.

The mental component of mitzvah is expressed by the Hebrew word *kavanah,* meaning intention, attention, devotion. *Kavanah* comes from the root k-v-n, to direct or aim. We send our actions out into the world deliberately, with purpose. Repetition does not equate with mindlessness: we try to put our heart into it every time. A toddler asks us to read a story for the umpteenth time. It may be the last thing we feel like doing right now. But because of our love for the child, we put as much feeling and genuine expression into each new performance as we can summon at that moment. So it is with mitzvot. We try to achieve a conscious performance.

We're not talking merely about dragging our focus back to the present moment, but about repeating an action until we can transcend "technique" and rise to a higher level. If you have ever devoted yourself to learning a musical instrument, or a craft like calligraphy or pottery, or a sport or martial art, you will get the sense here. The perfect golf or tennis swing comes only after a thousand swings; the perfect yoga pose after a thousand poses; the perfect earthenware pot after a thousand pots. We practice again and again until we are entrained, until the action wears a smooth and nearly effortless groove upon our bodies and hearts and minds. Only then can our controlling faculties relax and we can perform the action in harmony with the universe. So with mitzvot do we strive to act mindfully and in harmony each time. Of course we fall short of our aspirations, as we do in any practice we take up seriously. But without the striving we'd never make it at all.

I've had occasion to remember Reb Elimelekh's advice in my own life. Many years ago, for example, when I was a young rabbi in a synagogue in New England, my parishioners asked me to conduct services in English. I was taken aback at first, but I figured I could do English as well as the next guy, so I started leading prayers in English, complete with responsive readings. For some reason a line from Psalm 92 always comes to mind when I remember those days: "THOU HAS EXALTED MY POWER LIKE THAT OF A WILD OX," always in stentorian tones. For me this was davening like ersatz Episcopalians, so I would daven at home for myself first, then go off to synagogue to lead the prayers. The only trouble was that at home I was rushing to get to the synagogue, and at the synagogue, not only was I chanting in English, but I'd already davened for myself and was therefore not expressing the needs of my soul. I wasn't davening to God.

Then I remembered the advice of Reb Elimelekh of Lizhensk, and I realized that there was only one way I would learn to really talk to God in English. For the next forty days, even when I was davening for myself at home, I said everything in English, from the first word to the last. And little by little it started to work. After a few weeks, I could sing "Blessed art thou, O Lord, who healest the sick of thy people Israel" and *feel* it. Some months later I no longer felt the need to daven at home first. And to this day I'm still working on translations of our prayers that will flow naturally and allow us to praise God and express the yearning of our hearts in everyday English.

Another feature that strikes us immediately about mitzvot is their pervasiveness and level of detail. The details can seem fussy and arcane, but they are rooted in a place of love. The rabbis who elaborated on the basic mitzvot of the written Torah felt the same yearning that we feel today:

"If only my life had more meaning."

"I wish I acted more consciously, instead of just doing every-thing automatically, rushing through my day."

They knew how everyday distractions get in the way of ful-filling that yearning. Their ambition was to turn their entire life-space over to God. Since the Temple was destroyed, the sages said, the Holy One has no more space in this world than the four ells (a measure equivalent to the space occupied by a single body) marked out by each life lived under the compunction of divine commandment. You might say that they approached the problem as spiritual engineers. To lead a more conscious life, they were saying, we need to break down our lives into their constituent components—the moments that make up our days, the days that make up our years—and strive to live each moment as consciously as possible. "God," as the Rebbe of Kotzk taught centuries later, "resides wherever God is let in."

The mitzvot mark out spiritual territory in both time and space. That is why responding to a sense of being commanded can be paradoxically liberating. The mitzvot help us define parts of our lives in which we say: I dedicate this time to spiritual prac-tice. I take on this practice of my own free will. Nobody is forc-ing me, or urging me, or luring me into it. This is my decision.


## GETTING PAST THE GATEKEEPER


Ram Dass once said that from an economic point of view, India is a developing country; from a spiritual perspective, the United States is a developing country. Western society is heavily in-vested in intellect, less in emotions, and very little in spirituality.

Our language reveals this. We have a whole dictionary of words for reason, fantastic vocabularies and constructs with which to express our ideas. Our vocabulary of emotion is poorer, and our vocabulary of spirituality poorest of all. Open any good newspaper and you will find an article that will get your mind going, but only much more rarely do we find a contemporary piece of writing that really touches our hearts or exalts our spirits.

That is because something that would truly touch our souls must penetrate beyond the level of day-to-day understanding, beyond the fundamental barrier of logical thinking. It is as if our souls were waiting for us, yearning for us, in some inner courtyard, but the gate to that courtyard is guarded by a gatekeeper who rarely sleeps. A great deal of spiritual technology that religions have developed over time is designed to help us bypass that gatekeeper. Weighing such practices logically allows our critical faculties to judge precisely those methods that are designed to *circumvent* those faculties.

Ritual can seem forced and hollow to the logical mind. "This doesn't make sense," reason complains. "What am I doing this for?" But the limited reach of our logical minds is why ritual is so powerful. Feelings are stored and recalled through ritual. On our wedding anniversary we might buy flowers, dress up, and go out to a candlelight dinner to reexperience something of that special day when we said the words that bonded us to each other. Similarly, ritual can play an important part in conveying and reliving spiritual experiences. On Passover we try to recall the original experience of liberation from slavery through the extended ritual of the Seder. With the ritual greeting at Easter—

"Christ has risen"; "Indeed, he has risen"—Christians celebrate not only that Jesus rose on the third day but "He has risen in me, I've risen in Him"—now, today. The paradoxes, the inherent contradictions, the illogical demands that all religions include are a signal that our intellects are being asked to lie down so that our hearts and souls can listen.

A religion is a many-layered thing. It has developed the tools to touch the minds, hearts, and souls of all kinds of people, from toddler to elder, in happy times and sad, from ancient times to today. Think of our texts. We have stories that can enchant a four-year-old: the Garden of Eden, the story of Noah, Jonah and the whale. We have psalms we turn to in times of loss. We have erotic love poetry like the Song of Songs and books such as Job that have kept philosophers busy for centuries. The same many-layered approach applies to the mitzvot. Some mitzvot will seem logical to us; others are designed to appeal to our emotional and spiritual selves—which requires that they get around our intellect first. Repetition, ritual, and the very logic-shattering quality of these mitzvot are precisely what enables them to affect us on ever deeper levels.

Torah speaks of three categories of mitzvot: *mishpatim, edot,* and *chukim.* Loosely speaking we might translate *mishpatim* as ethical commandments, injunctions that appeal to our logical or intellectual faculties. *Edot* (or *eduyot,* as the word is rendered today) are historical, or "witnessing," commandments, which create and maintain our sense of memory and identity as a people. And *chukim* are ritual commandments, which defy explanation or logic to strike at our very souls. In truth each type of commandment

affects every faculty, but we can think of the three categories
as penetrating ever deeper into our being. Let us examine each
in turn.

## ACTS OF JUSTICE

*Mishpat* means justice. *Mishpatim* (the plural) set out the
boundaries of decent human behavior. The mitzvot in this category are simple, basic morality. As a citizen of this planet, Torah
seems to say, this is what you have to honor: Do not kill. Do not
steal. Help those less fortunate than yourself. Treat properly those
who work for you. Treat animals properly. Administer justice
impartially.

These mitzvot seem to represent the earliest sense our tradition had of what will lead society toward the *menschlichkeit* (human decency) we were trying to build. It was clear to us that
murder, incest, adultery, thievery, and false justice were not the
way to go. These are not laws in the sense of legislation so much
as universal laws of human discourse, which we have played a
part in discovering. *Mishaptim* invite us to add a level of intentionality to acts of human decency that we already do every day.
They are like little consciousness hooks upon which we can
hang the daily deeds we do for our own and the common good.

*Mishpatim* travel well. They are the most easily "portable"
into the modern world because they are based on what has become—thanks to mitzvot like these and similar injunctions in
other religions—simple common sense. Their sense is relatively

easy to preserve even when circumstances change, because the
same moral imperative that was beaming down to us when we
first subscribed to them is still beaming down to us today. Prohibitions against thievery or murder or bearing false witness are
timeless.

We can update other *mishpatim* by adopting the strategy of
the Jewish Reconstructionist movement, deconstructing the original intent of the mitzvah, then reconstructing it for the modern
era. For example: In biblical times, when the average person
lived in a mud brick house, they spent a great deal of time on the
roof. The Torah therefore commands us (Deuteronomy 22:8) to
put a parapet or railing on the roof of every house we build,
"that thou bring not blood upon your house, should any person
fall from there." *Ma'akeh*, a word that appears nowhere else in
the Bible besides this verse from Deuteronomy, means a railing,
restraint. What does that bring to mind today? Seat belts! To the
Jewish mind, the donning of a seat belt—a restraint designed to
save lives—is a mitzvah. We might even institute a blessing for
such safety measures, "Blessed are you, our God, King of the
Universe, who sanctified us with His commandments and commanded us with the mitzvah of *ma'akeh*." Such a blessing would
give a transpersonal or transcendent sense even to such an everyday
act. It is not only for my own safety that I put on the seat belt: I
want to connect this to the greater body of *mishpatim*. I want to
bring God into this level of my life, the level at which our tradition is urging us, as any parent would: "Take care of yourself."

Surely, we might think, we're quite capable of looking out
for ourselves on such a basic level without religion's getting in-

volved? Then we remember what a holy war Ralph Nader had
to wage to force automobile manufacturers to install seat belts.
Thanks to this understanding of the preservation of human life
as a higher calling, we are all safer today.

This is an example of how Torah can grow to embrace new
elements in our environment. The concern for protecting life is
not new. "The whole Law may be set aside for the saving of a
life," as a famous rabbinical injunction puts it. Here the old principle has a new investment in modern life—an application to
the automobile. Any act that protects life is sacred. Technology
that is dedicated to life-saving purposes acquires sanctity as well,
and its use becomes a holy act.

We connect with this holiness every time we lift our gaze
from our immediate self-interest to the public good. Washing your
hands before you cook is a greater mitzvah than washing your
hands before you eat: more people are involved. If we avoid jaywalking across a dangerous intersection, that's good. If we avoid
jaywalking across even a quiet intersection in order to set an example for a child who may be watching, that's better. The Torah
is amazingly detailed in its outlook on this level. When you go
to the bathroom, the Torah commanded the Israelites, take a little shovel and clean up after yourselves, "that your encampment
should be holy" (Deuteronomy 23:15). It is an amazingly early
example of environmental consciousness, one we will get back
to in chapter 5.

## DOORWAY: IT'S A MITZVAH

The next time you find yourself doing one of those common acts of human decency—something as simple as giving another driver the right of way, or calling a cheerful greeting to an elderly neighbor, or writing a check to your favorite charity—try saying to yourself, "It's a mitzvah. This act is meaningful. My act will—in no matter how small a way—change the world."

This refers to acts you *refrain* from doing in the name of human decency as well. Refraining from gossip, for instance, is a big topic in Jewish books of ethics. In Israel devout people often hang up a picture of the Chofetz Chayim, author of a famous work about guarding one's tongue, near the telephone. *Not* passing on that juicy tidbit you just learned about your coworker is surprisingly difficult, but it has cosmic significance. By letting even one thread of mildly malicious talk stop with you, you have improved the world.

A man came to the Chofetz Chayim once and told him that he wanted to do *t'shuvah* (to repent) from saying bad things about people, and that he needed help. "I'll show you how to do that," the Chofetz Chayim said, "if you bring me a pillow." When the man brought him a pillow, the Chofetz Chayim cut the pillow open, then leaned out the window and let the feathers fly where they would. "When you have brought all the feathers back and returned them to the pillow," the Chofetz Chayim told him, "you will have done t'shuvah for your deeds." Watching the feathers swirl away, far beyond his control, the man broke down in tears, realizing the immensity of what he had done.

Committing acts of kindness and refraining from acts of unkindness are mitzvot. Treasure them.

## ACTS OF WITNESSING

*Edut* is from the root meaning "to witness." If *mishpatim* are acts of the here and now, an *edut* (plural: *eduyot*) is an act of memory—historical memory, communal memory, sometimes even eternal memory.

I don't work on the Sabbath. Why? Because on Shabbos I bear witness that God is the Creator. Of course a day of rest makes sense as a *mishpat* as well, but the reason given in Torah is "For in six days God made the heavens, the earth, the sea, and all that they contain, and rested on the seventh day. Therefore God blessed the Sabbath day and made it holy" (Exodus 20:11). This takes it to another level. Keeping the Sabbath is not only a matter of taking care of ourselves. We are bearing witness to a dynamic of activity and rest, a yin and yang of movement and stasis, that is woven into the very fabric of the universe.

On Passover I bear witness to a monumental event in our mythic history: the freeing of the Children of Israel from slavery in Egypt. We place ourselves in the position of enslavement once again by avoiding leavened bread and eating what the Torah describes as the bread of impoverishment: matzoh. We eat bitter herbs, dip greens in salt water, place a sacrificial bone on our Seder plate, and sing songs of thanks to God. We do not dispense with this mitzvah, this witnessing, merely because archaeology assures us that the Exodus never happened as described. We bear witness to liberation from slavery—physical, mental, emotional, spiritual—as an eternal principle. At any time I wish to free myself of enslavement, I can connect to this affirmation and be liberated again from whatever Egypt enslaves me at this moment.

*Eduyot* generally involve ritual and often ask us to do things that are beyond the realm of common sense. I remember in 1969 I was busy getting ready for Passover, annihilating any traces of *chametz* (leavening) in my oven with a blowtorch, as is the custom in strictly traditional households these days, when the doorbell rang. It was Rabbi Arthur Green. Art would later become president of the Reconstructionist Rabbinical College, a professor at Brandeis, and dean of the rabbinical school at Hebrew College. At that time, though, he was busy setting up Havurat Shalom, one of the earliest of the grassroots davening circles that blossomed into the Havurah movement. Art wanted to borrow the blowtorch when I was finished. In those days we were hot on radical theology, talking about the death of the ancient names of God, how they all needed to be reconfigured. "Why are we doing this?" Art wondered aloud as he waited for me to finish. "Aren't we radical theologians?" But we both knew that, yes, we considered ourselves radical theologians and yet Art still wanted the blowtorch to kosher his oven. The bearing of witness cannot be done lightly.

The more elaborate and dedicated our performance of *eduyot,* the more they sustain us. One of the injunctions in Torah regarding the commandments is *lishmor*—to guard and to keep. We got the clear sense that by keeping the *mishpatim* we are in turn looking out for ourselves, both practically and spiritually. Similarly, when we bear witness through our performance of *eduyot* the effort we expend repays itself, but on a deeper level. That is why I believe so strongly that *eduyot* call for firsthand involvement, the more elaborate the better. On Passover I used to pick dandelion greens to use for bitter herbs. For Hanukkah one year I bought twenty pounds of olives to make olive oil for the menorah. I didn't really understand what needs to be done, so I made a big mess and got only four nights' worth of oil, but the experience of *doing* it was so much more powerful than just opening those little boxes of colored candles. Creative involvement, to me, is more important than observing the rituals to the letter. I once made a mezuzah from one of those tiny recording devices they were putting in greeting cards for a while so you could record little messages for grandma's birthday. Every time I touched the button I heard my own voice remind me: "Wake up as you pass this threshold."

The more we get involved in observing the *eduyot,* the more power we invest in them. Conversely, the less we are involved, the more we rob these mitzvot of their power to move us. Take the mitzvah of tzitzit, for example, the white, knotted tassles that appear at each corner of the tallis (prayer shawl) and on simpler four-cornered garments that Orthodox men wear under their clothes. The third and last paragraph of the *Shema* is devoted to the witness of tzitzit, "so that you will look upon it and remember God's commands." Since time immemorial, wearing tzitzit has helped us define our personal space as sacred space. To the modern mind, of course, they seem anachronistic, a throwback to much earlier times. Some synagogues have dispensed with prayer shawls altogether. In others Jews stand uncomfortably with the little blue and white "bikinis" draped around their necks like scarves. Only in traditional venues do you see people swaying under full-sized prayer shawls wrapped around them like robes, tossed back over their shoulders or draped over their heads as hoods to enclose them in a space of inner prayer. And yet very few even among the Orthodox learn to tie their own tzitzit. To me that's like hiring a contractor to buy a mezuzah and put it on my house instead of nailing it in myself. With a store-bought solution I lose an opportunity for personal transformation. No wonder tzitzit seem silly to some of us.

And yet my experience is that children, especially, love to get involved in these things if given half the chance. In New Bedford, Massachusetts, I was in charge of the Jewish Scouts. Since scouts have to do all kinds of knots, I showed them how to do the knots of the tzitzit and tefillin (phylacteries). When I served as "religious environmentalist" at Camp Ramah, I solicited textile remnants from manufacturers and created a "tallisarium," with a sewing machine and a serger, or hemming machine. The kids came in, chose their cloth, sewed it up, put corners on it, and then tied their own *tzitzit* in each corner.

We might gaze reverently at the power objects of indigenous and shamanistic societies, forgetting that our own tradition has developed such technology as well. I once went to an interfaith gathering of mystics and philosophers in Calgary. We stayed in a generic modern hotel downtown and were scheduled to begin our meetings at breakfast. I got up before dawn to daven, but the hotel room didn't feel like the right ambience, so I went upstairs and found a trapdoor that led out to the roof. I stepped out, surrounded by chimneys and vents, found a corner, took out my tallis and tefillin and siddur and prepared myself for prayer. Five minutes later the trapdoor opened again and up came Brother Rufus Goodstriker, a Blood Indian. We nodded to each other. Brother Rufus found his own corner, unpacked his prayer blanket, lit a little fire, and offered up some herbs. So we said our prayers, he in his corner, me in mine. The sun was rising over the prairie to the east, the alpenglow was lighting up the Rocky Mountains to the west. Just as the sun came over the horizon, Brother Rufus blew an eagle bone whistle in all four directions to greet it. Since it was shortly before the High Holy Days, I took out my ram's horn and gave a blow, too, as is the Jewish custom.

After we had finished Brother Rufus came over to me. "May I see your instruments?" he asked. "I wasn't home," he added, "so I couldn't take a sweat, but I took a shower this morning instead." If I'm going to touch someone else's spiritual instruments, he was saying, I should be ritually clean. He picked up my tefillin first. "Rawhide," he noted. He noticed they were sewn together with natural gut and nodded. He looked carefully at the knots and ran his fingers over them slowly. "Noble knots," he said. Next he shook the tefillin's headpiece and heard something move. "What's inside the black box?" A piece of parchment, I told him, on which was written holy texts with God's name. He nodded. He picked up the shofar and looked it over. "Ram's horn," he said, blew a few loud notes, and handed it back. "Much better than cow." Then he examined the knotted fringes at the corner of my tallis, each with five double knots interspersed with columns of wound thread. "What's the message?" he asked.

I told him a story from the Talmud. Once there was a Jewish man who was always careful to wear his tzitzit but was perhaps less vigilant with other commandments. This man hears of a courtesan so skilled and beautiful that she charges 400 golden dinars for her hire. So he sends her 400 golden dinars and makes an appointment. At the appointed time he appears at her door, where the maid announces him and shows him into the courtesan's room. There he sees seven beds. The first six were made of silver: on these the courtesan would arouse her clients. On the seventh bed, which was made entirely of gold, the affair would be consummated.

The courtesan lay before him, naked. Overcome with desire he rushed over to sit beside her, shedding his own garments— but just then, the Talmud tells, his tzitzit rose up and hit him in the face. He slipped off the bed and sat on the floor. Immediately the courtesan slipped off the bed as well and sat down next to him. "What have I done to displease you?" she asked. "What blemish have you seen in me? I will not rest until you tell me."

"I have never seen a woman as lovely as you," the man replied. "But only one commandment do I really fulfill, and that is the wearing of these fringes here, the tzitzit. Now my tzitzit have risen up against me as witnesses: I cannot carry out this act."

The courtesan was astounded. She had never seen such restraint. "I will not leave you," she said, "until you tell me your name, where you are from, and the name of your teacher and the school at which you study." And so he wrote down these things on a piece of paper and handed it to her.

The courtesan rose and divided her fortune into three parts. One she gave to the poor, one she paid as taxes, and one she kept, along with the beautiful sheets from her golden bed. Then she went to the *bet midrash* (house of study) of Rabbi Chiyya, as written on the paper. "Teach me, Master," she said. "I wish to convert."

Rabbi Chiyya was confused. "Perhaps you have set your eyes on one of my disciples?" he asked. Then she told him the story and showed him the paper, whereupon he agreed to teach her. "Now go," he said to her, "and enjoy what you have acquired by your action." And so, the Talmud tells us, the very sheets she had spread out in preparation for the illicit union with her client she soon spread out for him lawfully as his wife.

Brother Rufus loved the story and understood it. He had examined my ritual objects with the same reverence and respect that we might reserve for, say, Native American prayer objects. He understood that these are not just mumbo jumbo from a distant past. They have meaning and power to this very day—if we let them.

The third paragraph of the *Shema*, where we express the commandment of tzitzit, brings up another dimension of the *eduyot,* the witnessing mitzvot. "God spoke to Moses, saying: Speak to the children of Israel and tell them to make fringes on the corners of their garments *le-dorotam,* for their generations" (Numbers 15:37). We can understand this expression to mean that we should do this same practice in every generation. But it has another connotation as well: "Do this *on behalf* of your [future] generations." If we sense and believe that our tradition has value, that it is a treasure worth passing on to future generations as it has somehow been passed on to us, the witnessing commandments are particularly valuable here. The *mishpatim,* as I said, are closer to simple common sense. But bearing public witness to the eternal principles and experiences of our people—that is what enables each generation to pass our tradition on to the next.

The word *le-dorotam* also appears in the kiddush, the blessing over the wine, that we would traditionally say on Sabbath morning upon returning from synagogue. *"Ve-shamru benei Yisrael et ha-Shabbat*—And the children of Israel kept and preserved the Shabbat—*le-dorotam,* through and on behalf of all future generations, *b'rit olam,* as a covenant forever."

Witnessing and memory. The opportunity for creative involvement. A call to consciousness. A message from the past to the present and into the future. *Eduyot* like Shabbat and tzitzit embody all these ideas. Am I saying that you should walk around with the fringes peeping out from under your shirt, like the ultra-Orthodox? Not necessarily. But I *would* encourage you to adopt some form of tzitzit at least on a *metaphorical* level, to take on— when you're ready—Jewish practices that resonate with you in the way that *eduyot* are meant to. The fringes on the corner of the garment have no practical purpose. We don't tie them together to keep the garment in place, or hang our keys or cell phones from them. What they do is add a dimension of consciousness beyond the shopping-mall mentality, beyond that of our everyday grind. If we surround ourselves with this extra dimension, as the tzitzit surround us in all four directions, we will add value to our lives and, God willing, the lives of our children as well.

Think of the Seder. The Seder is probably the most brilliant technology our tradition has developed for witnessing and transmission. The *Haggadah,* or Seder liturgy, expressly dedicates itself to getting the children involved in witnessing our deliverance from slavery to freedom. This multidimensional family celebration is one of Judaism's greatest teaching tools, one we can offer to the rest of the world. As I relate later in chapter 6, I suggested the Seder to the Dalai Lama as a way to help preserve the Tibetan nation and religion in exile. Before the Chinese robbed you of your homeland, I told him, it was easier to pass on your culture and beliefs to your children's children's children. Now that you're in the Diaspora, you need to create and maintain a *portable* homeland, a shared cognitive space, that every Tibetan family can relate to and participate in. The things that are *le-dorotam,* that you do on behalf of future generations, become of supreme importance. Why not use the Seder as a model?

We need to remember that children are more receptive to ceremony and ritual than many adults. Small children, especially, are not as concerned with those aspects that we consider archaic, that we think are not in keeping with modern sensibilities. For children the main question is whether it's fun, whether they can participate, and whether there's a story involved—and they don't expect stories of the same factual level as we read in the newspaper, but rather myths and fairy tales. *The Prince of Egypt* is a marvelous animated rendering of the Exodus story: kids get totally swept up in it—and so do adults, if we allow ourselves to be! The ages before the critical intellect is well developed are the best ages to present the more archaic material: those ages provide a fertile ground in which to plant seeds that can be very meaningful later in life. So I'm in favor of pushing the archaic things more for those of tender years.

## ACTS OF MYSTERY

*Chok* (plural *chukim*) is the deepest level of mitzvah and the hardest level to understand. *Chok* means law or decree and comes from the root meaning engraved. These are the laws that are carved in stone. A Hasidic interpretation imagines the three levels like this. *Mishpatim,* the logical injunctions, are like letters written on plastic. They are legible and clear; they leap to the eye and the mind. Yet they are easy to wipe off and rewrite. *Eduyot,* the witnessing commandments, are like writing in indelible ink. They are not so easy to wipe away: something always remains. And yet they, too, could fade after long exposure to the sun. *Chukim* are engraved, chipped out of stone with a hammer and chisel. They can't be wiped off, nor will they fade. The letters may get filled up and obscured, but as soon as you wash them off their message reveals itself again.

In order to transmit an engraved message, the medium of transmission must give up something of itself: this is what the chipping-out process of engraving entails. And the medium of transmission here is *us*. More than the other types of mitzvot, the *chukim* ask for a higher level of surrender to a will that is not our own. Though *chukim* can be so hard to accept, they are also the level of mitzvah that I would be most afraid to tamper with, for I have found that they touch much deeper, preverbal levels in me than *mishpatim* and *eduyot*. They bring me closer to the realization of God. As sorely tempted as we may be sometimes to rewrite or simply jettison these mitzvot altogether, I don't think any practice we would make up today—having vetted it for respectability and conformation to our modern views—could touch us in so deep a way.

Circumcision is perhaps the best-known example of a *chok*. Yes, the Torah commands us to perform the bris as a sign for all time of our covenant with God, so it has aspects of *edut* as well. But all the explanations and all the meanings shatter at the rock of "How can I do this to my son?" This practice cannot be logically defended. I have such trouble with it, have wrestled with it, and yet I feel more commanded with this than I feel with any other mitzvah. I couldn't do it unless I felt so commanded. It counters so many things that I believe—yet I'm convinced that the transmission would be lost for uncircumcised Jews, that we would lose them. This is raw soul to raw body, without the mind intercepting.

Emotions often take over when we perform one of these *mitzvot*. Imagine a modern Jewish couple who give birth to a boy. For days they anguish over the question, "Should we have him circumcised?" Often their extreme ambivalence results in a compromise, and the boy is circumcised at the hospital by a surgeon, sometimes without even the parents in attendance. But if after much hesitation and soul searching the parents of the newborn summon the *mohel* and gather their family and friends about them; if they say, in effect, "We stand before our loved ones and the greater community, as our ancestors did before us, to submit to a mystery that is beyond our power to understand"; if they choose to consciously forge another link in a chain that goes back a hundred generations to the dawn of history—then you will often see hearts break open in a mix of joy and sorrow, fear and relief. The relinquishing of power that takes place with the fulfillment of a *chok* can open us up and touch us to a depth that we cannot attain unless we somehow allow this state of vulnerability. Such a realization can earn even the *chukim* the consent of our minds as well as our souls.

Other *chukim* summon a similar sense of mystery and power. Why should the shofar be made of ram's horn? Few less sophisticated instruments exist even in the world's most primitive societies. We could make the most beautiful and awesome music with synthesizers and sound systems—but the *shofar*-ness is not going to happen. Those blasts on Rosh ha-Shanah and Yom Kippur transport us back to an ancient and primal place.

My own most powerful experience of blowing the shofar took place over sixty years ago, and here again, the aspect of firsthand involvement was crucial. It was 1940; I was just sixteen years old. My family, having fled from Austria after its annexation by Nazi Germany, were considered enemy aliens by the French, and we were placed in a detention camp in southern France. We had been able to communicate with the American consulate in Marseilles and were waiting anxiously for visas to emigrate to the States.

We had been in southern France about three or four weeks, Rosh ha-Shanah was approaching, but we had no *sefer Torah*, we had *nothing*. I'd heard there was a butcher in town and thought maybe I could get a ram's horn from him, so one morning I snuck out of the camp at around five in the morning and went to find him. He was killing goats and thought I wanted some meat. I told him no, I wanted a horn. He gave me two, with the skull bones still attached, which I took back to the camp. I got some charcoal from leftover fires that people built to cook with, put the horns with the bones in a can full of water, and boiled them until I could pull the bones out. By this time I had sharpened a wire hanger by rubbing it on a rock, and I pushed it and twisted it, pushed it and twisted it. It took a long time, but finally, just before Rosh ha-Shanah, I managed to drill through one of the horns.

Everyone gathered around, and I raised the shofar to my lips and blew. The commandant came in with his whip and an automatic and asked what all the noise was. "*C'est le cornet de notre libération, monsieur le commandant,*" I said. It's the trumpet of our liberation.

"*Notre libération?*" he said. "*Quelle chance,*" what a coincidence—and he told me to tootle it again. I gave another blow, whereupon he pulled out a letter and read the names of the people whose visas were waiting for them at the American embassy in Marseilles. Our family was among them.

THE JEWISH WAY of mitzvah, then, encompasses actions that speak to different levels of our psyches. Logical, balanced, healthy action has a place. Ritual in which we join together in collective witnessing of eternal principles has a place. And decrees that we submit to out of a sense of mystery and even bafflement—these, too, have a place. Judaism, like all world religions, recognizes that if we are to be transformed, we must appeal not only to the head, but penetrate to our hearts and to our very souls as well.

## TASTE AND SEE

Taking up a practice is not easy. The decision is not one we can just slide under our psyche's radar screen, hoping it will just happen without conscious commitment. We must first make what Hebrew calls a *haskamah she-ba-lev,* an agreement in our heart—*with* our heart—that this is important, that we're actually going to do this. We need an inner "Yes." Just as we might decide that our physical health is something we need to set aside time and money for, we have to budget for soul stuff. We have to set aside soul dollars and soul hours, even perhaps soul days every once in a while.

Of course we will need to recommit ourselves many times after that first "Yes." Judaism is not a religion of saints: it understands the difficulty of changing one's behavior, of raising the bar for oneself. The Hasidim tell of Reb Levi Yitzchak of Berditchev, who used to say, before he went to sleep at night, "Master of the Universe, today I didn't do so well. I promise that tomorrow I'm going to do better."

Immediately he would chide himself. "But Levi Yitzchak, that's what you said last night!"

"Ah, but tonight," he'd reply to himself, "*tonight* I really mean it."

It's a beautiful teaching tale. We have no better way to overcome the sabotaging that we do to ourselves—to our own best-laid plans!—than to try to adjust the "I mean it" a little each day. Each day, we unravel one more particle of the self-sabotage.

Levi Yitzchak's inner review is itself a Jewish practice called *cheshbon nefesh*. This translates literally into keeping the soul's accounts, examining the soul's balance sheet. The closing moments of our day, before we go to sleep, are a marvelous time for this reexamination and rededication. In the evening, as often as you can, gently review your day. How did it go? Did you rise to the standard you set for yourself? Where did you fall short, and how might you do better?

Inevitably we will lose our initial enthusiasm: we will feel stuck; our practice will seem empty. At these times it might help to remember that Judaism is perfectly content to allow our *kavanah,* our inspiration and intention, to catch up to our physical actions when necessary. Continue your practice and stay open; *kavanah* will return. Reb Nachman of Bratslav had a wonderful teaching of how soul and body help each other with this. The soul should teach the body all the good things it learns, Reb Nachman teaches, for there will be times when the soul will feel depressed, when it just won't have access to that uplifted feeling it needs so much. Then it will be able to come to the body and say, "Will you please remind me? What does it feel like?" Whereupon the body can repeat the actions it has learned as many times as it takes, until the soul recovers that feeling of connection.

Remember, too, that anything we do happens on so many different levels. Imagine four Jews from the legendary shtetl of Chelm, the world capital of Jewish foolishness, bickering over who is the better Jew. "Some people only go to synagogue on Shabbos," the first boasts, "but I go every day. I'm seven times more Jewish than they are."

"Yeah, yeah," says the second. "But I've seen you daven. You daven with your little finger. I might not show up every time, but when I daven, I really daven."

"Sure you do," says the third. "You moan like a cow and *shokl* sway like a weed in the wind. You make God deaf already, with all your noise! But when it comes to dealing with *people,* all that righteousness goes right out the window."

"Oh, be quiet, all of you," scoffs the fourth, "with your davening and your *mitzvos*—and no more thought involved than if you were peeling potatoes. The hands move, the legs move, the mouth moves—but the head and the heart? They're at home under the bed."

As so often happens, the wise men of Chelm are actually on to something. Frequency, intensity, range, consciousness—each of these is an important part of practice, and each can provide us with a focus for the day. As a beautiful verse from the *Haftarah* of the Noah portion urges: *"harchivi mekom ohalayikh"* (Isaiah 54:2). Make your dwelling place more spacious. Expand the reach of your spiritual tent. We have so many ways to increase the Yiddishkeit in our lives, to enhance whatever practice we've taken upon ourselves. We might decide to devote a little more time: if we were going to synagogue on High Holy Days only, we might go for a Friday night service once a month as well. We might decide to extend our range, from giving money to charity to volunteering occasionally at a local soup kitchen. We might look for ways to intensify our practice, inviting friends to our Friday night meal or singing songs with our children. We might study or meditate to add a higher degree of consciousness to something we're already doing.

Pay attention to what gives you the greatest mileage. If you're an intellectual person, you need new ideas. If you're an emotional person, what songs or poetry move you most? If you're a person who needs a deep sense of rootedness, myths and stories can help. If you're a pursuer of justice, find a cause to get involved in.

Like Reb Levi Yitzchak, we can use our capacity for internal dialogue to strengthen our resolve each time, taking a minute before starting our practice for an internal dialogue that goes something like this.

—Ready to begin my practice for today?

—Ready.

—Ready to invest some energy?

—Ready.

—Ready to improve my life and the world in some small way?

—Ready.

—Ready to relax into what I'm about to do, to open my heart as wide as possible, to welcome something of that universal presence?

—Ready.

When we finish we do the opposite. We give thanks for whatever we have experienced and ask ourselves:

—Ready to bring a tiny spark of holiness back to our everyday world?

—Ready.

Approach this with a sense of experiment. The Orthodox world I grew up in believed that the Torah and the Rabbis had already told us the right way to do things: no sense of experiment was necessary. The truth is that our people has always been experimenting, for that's how societies evolve: through trial and error.

But tradition downplays the evolution of Jewish practice through the ages, since this seems to challenge the tradition's claim to eternal truth. When such evolution is too obvious to deny, tradition claims divine guidance. Divinely guided we may have been—but this does not negate the continuous experimentation, adjusting, and readjusting that our people has engaged in over the centuries.

Today we are less interested in what the tradition dictates than in *what works*. How we put our spiritual realization into practice is up to each soul to decide. If a given practice interests you or an opportunity for Yiddishkeit presents itself, try it. If it doesn't work, try something else. But remember that the less logical the mitzvah, the deeper it can reach. Rather than merely staying with a practice you can live with logically, push yourself a little. Listen to your heart as much as you can. Try to go with what gives you chills or goose bumps, or what makes you laugh or cry. That's where the power is.

# PART TWO

# THE TORAH
# OF TOMORROW

CHAPTER 5

# A NEW KIND OF KOSHER

J UDAISM is like an ancient tree. The core of any mature tree is old wood. The old wood is crucial to
maintaining the tree's structure, its ability to withstand
the changing winds, but no growth is going on there. The living processes that are the *growth* of the tree, its message to the future, take place only in the tree's newest and outermost ring.

We today are that outermost ring, and the growing is up to
us. Of course we need to remember and understand our past as
we grow into the future. Any new growth must spring from the
DNA that created, and continues to create, the Jewish organism.
Our texts, our history, our stories, our traditions, are all part of
the fundamental blueprint of our faith. The better we learn to
listen to the voices of the past, the more we can learn of ancient
wisdom that, with a little imagination, is still precious and ap-
plicable today. But religion becomes oppressive when we have

too much preservation and not enough innovation. Some things the past cannot teach us. These we must learn from the present— our present—and our future. Our task as new cells is not to respond to the weather of yesteryear; we have to deal with the challenges of *today*.

As every page of the Talmud shows, we Jews have always learned by asking questions. The more we seek to learn, the bigger and more penetrating our questions must be. If we want a faith that will uphold not only the values of the past, but those of the present and future as well, we must ask: What are the most fundamental questions and issues of our age?

## THE EXUBERANT EARTH

Jews who are my age today have lived through two events that required entirely new ways of thinking, theological as well as practical. The first was the Holocaust. The Jews had been persecuted for centuries, but our people had not been threatened so directly with total annihilation since the Romans crushed the Judean revolts in the first and second centuries. Like the destruction of the Temple, the Holocaust struck not only at our bodies, but at our souls. How were we to understand a God whose plan for us included the organized slaughter of six million Jews?

The second was the birth of the State of Israel: no event since the building of the Second Temple had promised such resurrection in the face of catastrophe. Like the building of the Temples, the granting of our own state quickly brought painful clashes between holy aspirations and worldly, sometimes brutal, realities.

How do we, a terribly traumatized but now newly enfranchised people, live with one another and with the communities that surround us? How do we, as individuals, define ourselves in relation to the State of Israel? These are urgent questions: we have struggled with them for over half a century and are struggling still.

But the biggest question that the future is posing to us affects not only Jews but all the peoples of the world. This question, too, is posed by two great events that occurred within a single generation, the first heralding destruction, the second holding out the possibility of redemption. We witnessed the first event in the atomic mushroom cloud rising above the New Mexican desert, a sight physicist J. Robert Oppenheimer greeted with his famous reference to the Bhagavad Gita: "Now I am become Death, the destroyer of worlds." Hiroshima, Nagasaki, and the arms race followed. Terrible as the Holocaust was, the nuclear arms race threatened a Holocaust a thousand times bigger. For the first time in history we were faced with the possibility that all peoples, not just ours, might be annihilated—and by our own hand. Today it seems that this planeticide may not happen all at once, but little by little. This is no more comforting.

The second great event was the sight of our planet from outer space. "Viewed from the distance of the moon," the biologist Lewis Thomas wrote, "the astonishing thing about the earth, catching the breath, is that it is alive. The photographs show the dry, pounded surface of the moon in the foreground, dead as an old bone. Aloft, floating free beneath the moist, gleaming membrane of bright blue sky, is the rising earth, the only exuberant thing in this part of the cosmos." This one single vision represented an immense shift of perspective, beckoning us to rise beyond social, political, cultural, or religious formulations of "us versus them." It clarified better than a thousand words how much humanity as a whole has to lose and how much our collective home is worth fighting for. The wonderful gift of life that our planet represents is so improbable: the harsh and silent surfaces of our nearest neighbors—the moon, Mars, Venus—represent the far more likely possibility. We knew these things intellectually, but the sight of our planet in all its loveliness said it more eloquently than any scientific data or idealistic sermon could.

To me, the sight of our Earth from outer space is not only a scientific triumph but today's most potent *religious* icon as well. More than I want to talk about *avodat ha-Shem,* serving God, I want to talk about serving the planet. In fact we can find places in Torah where the two imperatives clearly merge. Deuteronomy 30:19 lays out the choice clearly. "I call heaven and earth to witness to you this day: I have set before you life and death, the blessing and the curse. Choose life, so that you and your seed may live." On the one hand we have the threat of Earth's destruction, whether cataclysmic or gradual; on the other, we have the halting emergence of planetary cooperation, countries putting their heads together to control crime and disease, mediate conflict, and protect the environment. Strengthening this whole-Earth cooperation is to me the most urgent and important way we have of serving God, the holiest and most pressing invitation of our time.

The question is: can Judaism respond?

# DOORWAY:
# EARTH AS ICON

Take a few quiet moments, if you will, and make the following mind-journey with me.

Imagine yourself soaring over the vast plaza of the Western Wall, the Jewish people's holiest site. Below you, small dark figures walk or stand near the wall and sway. You see the men's and women's sections. Maybe someday there will be a place where both can pray together.

Now rise higher until you can see all of the Old City below you. If you know the lay of the land, you can pick out the different quarters—Jewish, Christian, Moslem. How these neighbors have fought over the centuries! How much blood has been spilled!

Keep rising, higher and higher, until you're at the level of satellite photos. In the center, still, is Israel. You can see the Moslem lands of North Africa and the Middle East and the Christian-dominated countries of Europe.

Keep rising outward and upward in your mind until finally, like an astronaut, you can picture our entire planet below you, suspended blue and lovely in space. Spend some time just gazing down at her from your position out in space. She looks so serene from here. Think of the expression "the Promised Land." Could this take on new meaning?

Now remember the verse that we sing in taking out the Torah: "*Etz chayim hi la-machazikim bah.* She is the Tree of Life to all who hold to her." Think of all the citizens of Earth around the globe, held to her surface by gravity's embrace. Can this phrase, too, take on new meaning?

## SEEDS OF A JEWISH ENVIRONMENTALISM

How are we, not just Jews but all the world's peoples, to live in our global home? We will need the insights of each and every faith community to answer this question. The world's religions have been slow to respond, but environmentalists of faith have been doing some creative thinking in recent years, led in the Jewish case by teachers like Rabbi Arthur Waskow. It turns out that Judaism's particular character gives us very firm ground to stand on as we struggle to respond to this question as Jews and in a deeply Jewish way.

Judaism has often been called a householder religion. World religions like Christianity, Hinduism, and Buddhism all had their own monastic or ascetic traditions, urging the best among them to renounce worldly concerns in their pursuit of the holy. The problem is that neither a priestly elite nor a class of monks has to take responsibility for how the world is run, for planting in spring and harvesting in the fall. Judaism, on the other hand, insists that we elevate our *everyday lives* to the sacred. Most of the mitzvot are aimed at ordinary people in ordinary situations. Even rabbis are encouraged to learn and practice a trade, get married, have children—to have a strong stake in the business of *life*.

What we see when we look around us depends on the glasses we're wearing. If we look at the world through the spectacles of a householder, the first thing we notice is what needs doing, what needs fixing up. The laws of Torah were concerned that the courts be impartial, public thoroughfares be safe, lost and stolen property returned, slaves treated properly, the poor taken care of. A householder religion can play a crucial role in the physical stewardship of the planet, for our spirituality is not ethereal or otherworldly but rather grounded in that very stewardship.

Our biblical ancestors had no concept of our Earth as a planet. Most would have lived and died in the same dusty landscape, within the span of a few weeks' camel walk at most. Yet Torah's worldview, advanced through very specific injunctions, presents a coherent and holistic vision that we might still envy today. Here are a few of the injunctions we encounter.

- Every seventh year you must let the land lie fallow, neither sowing nor harvesting crops.
- All bondsmen must be freed on the sabbatical year as well, and all loans forgiven.
- Land may not be sold in perpetuity; every fiftieth year, on the Jubilee, all fields must be restored to their ancestral owners.
- In harvesting your fields you must leave a corner for the poor, along with any sheaves that escape the harvester. In addition, you must give the poor a tenth of your harvest.

- You may not yoke a bull and an ass together, lest the smaller animal suffer.
- You may not intermingle two plant species in a single field: each genetic strain must remain inviolate.
- You must not slaughter an animal and its offspring in a single day, nor take a bird and its chicks at one time.

Given the limited horizons of life in biblical times, the ecological view of Torah is amazingly sophisticated. Torah makes no separation between the ecology of plants, of animals, and of people: the three are inseparable. The word *ecology* comes from the Greek word *oikos,* or house: it recognizes the world as our home, and studies how to live in it.

In Torah this home is defined as "the land that I have promised thee." Most of these mitzvot are called *mitzvot ha-t'luyot ba-aretz,* commandments that are dependent on "the Land," Eretz Yisrael. So now we are faced with two challenges. All the years that we lived in ghettoes, where we were not able to work the land, and in the Diaspora, where so many of these laws don't apply, have robbed us of the strong connection with the land and our *oikos,* our home. How can we recover that connection? And how can we expand our understanding of "the Land" to include the planet that all faiths share?

## A NEW KIND OF KOSHER

I was brought up in a strictly kosher home and was trained as a ritual slaughterer, so I was well versed in the basic Jewish practice of being discriminating about the food that I took into my body. But around thirty years ago I began wondering about questions that none of the volumes of laws and clarifications regarding kashrut seemed to deal with. As usual in Jewish law, these questions took off not from principles and generalities, but from specific instances. For example: Disposable dishes—a Styrofoam take-out container, say, or a nonrecyclable soft-drink bottle—are, from the perspective of classical *halakhah,* ideal. Since nobody has ever used them before, no suspicion exists that they've ever been touched by *trafe* food. From an ecological point of view, however—from the perspective of the human race and our overflowing landfills—they are disastrous. How to reconcile these two perspectives?

I began thinking of a new kind of kashrut, one that would combine the ancient ways of thoughtful consumption and avoidance of cruelty and violence with the new awareness of the wider repercussions of some of our actions, a way of thinking that I called *eco-kashrut.*

Once you start thinking this way, other questions quickly arise. What could be more kosher, for example, than potato latkes or potato kugel? Yet "the typical potato grower," author Michael Pollan writes in *The Botany of Desire,* "stands in the middle of a bright green circle of plants that have been doused with so much pesticide that their leaves wear a dull white chemical bloom and the soil they're rooted in is a lifeless gray powder." Is there a sense in which vegetables grown with such deadly methods are less kosher than we'd want them to be? What about irradiated vegetables or ones developed through genetic engineering? Given that beef takes so much more grazing land to produce than chicken, is there a sense in which chicken is more kosher? Is tuna fished from dangerously depleted stocks kosher? Such a line of thinking might easily be extended to products other than food. Is wood from nonrenewable forests kosher? Is electricity from nuclear power plants kosher?

Kashrut pays attention not only to the end results, but to the methods used to obtain them. According to tradition, the fruit of oppressed labor is just as tainted as meat from an animal that was slaughtered without mercy. Torah forbids us, as we have seen, to join an ox, a very large animal, and a donkey, a smaller, weaker animal, in the same harness. Are fruit and vegetables picked by underpaid migrant workers (as almost all produce in our country is) kosher? Are coffee beans from farmer-owned cooperatives more kosher than coffee from larger and more oppressive companies? Are sneakers or rugs created by slave or child labor kosher?

A practice of eco-kashrut adapts a very traditional Jewish way of asking consumption-related questions to the questions of our day. But it also differs from traditional kashrut in three important ways. First, eco-kashrut is concerned not only with the *origin* of the things consumed—what animal the meat came from, say, or what dishes it was cooked in—but also with the *results* of our consumption, such as the environmental and human toll of our actions.

Second, according to traditional laws of kashrut, either something is kosher or it isn't. More difficult cases might require that we turn to a rabbi with expertise in such matters, but his ruling will be either yes or no. Some Jews might hew to stricter definitions than others—consumers of glatt kosher food, for example, avoid any hint of a doubt that might arise in the status of even a properly slaughtered animal—but food in any given Orthodox setting is never "sort of kosher." An eco-kosher practice, however, cannot always make such cut-and-dried pronouncements. All consumption has multiple interlocking costs and repercussions. Our challenge is to *maximize* the kashrut of a given product or action—a matter of degree, rather than a question with a yes-or-no answer.

This brings us to the third difference. An eco-kosher practice is a matter of individual conscience and decision, rather than a matter of legislation. And it will be an evolving practice, as over the years our understanding of the laws of nature and the friendliness of our technology improves. Scientists will keep us informed, and ethicists or rabbis trained in the practice of eco-kashrut can help us sort out the results of our actions. But the day-to-day weighing of conflicting considerations, personal as well as social, environmental, and technological, is up to each of us.

## MESSAGES TO THE FUTURE

A practice of eco-kashrut is only one example of how Judaism can respond to one of the most urgent moral questions of our day. When we begin to dig deep in our tradition we find various intriguing *etzot*—advice, counsel, hints—that speak to this new challenge. Some of these sources have gone unemphasized for centuries. We should dust them off and reexamine them. Other gems, though in common circulation for much of our history, will quickly take on new and powerful hues when we hold them up to a different light.

*Spare that tree.* Let's look at one eco-friendly example that, like kashrut, was expanded well beyond its original intent of preserving an enemy's fruit trees in wartime.

> When you shall besiege a city many days, making war against it
> to take it, you shall not destroy its trees, wielding an axe upon
> them, for you may eat from them and shall not cut them down,
> for [is] a tree of the field [like] a man, to be besieged by you?
> (Deuteronomy 20:19)

We see from this passage that even in wartime, "slash and burn" or "scorched earth" policies were not tolerated. The rabbis greatly extended this principle: if in wartime such wanton destruction is forbidden, they said, how much more true must this be in ordinary circumstances! They therefore deduced the much more general principle of *bal tashchit* or "[do] not destroy," forbidding wanton destruction or wasteful consumption of any kind. The thirteenth-century *Sefer ha-Chinukh* (Book of Education), a classic survey of the 613 mitzvot, teaches that this includes any pointless destruction whatsoever, by burning, tearing, breaking, or any other means. Not even a mustard seed, the *Sefer ha-Chinukh* says, should be lost to this world without reason.

*Clean up after yourself.* Now take a small and very practical injunction that we find in Deuteronomy 23:14–15. When you go outside your encampment to relieve yourself, the Torah instructed, take a little shovel and cover your excrement with dirt afterward. Why? Because the Lord thy God walks with you in your camp, so keep your encampment holy.

From this we see that our ancestors, too, were conscious of the quality of their surroundings. It's not hard to see how such awareness can be extended. Today we have a far less localized vision of God. God's presence—and thus, by extension, the camp— is everywhere. Our idea of waste has expanded, too. The injunction to "keep your encampment holy" extends to any waste we produce, everywhere we live. The Torah's message, both as individuals and as a society, is clear: Don't forget to clean up your mess. Hasten its return to the earth. And do it out of a sense of higher purpose. Here is an amazingly early example of environmental awareness, implying that any measure we take to curb pollution is a holy act.

## SEEING WITH THE EYES OF WISDOM

Judaism's down-to-earth, practical teachings are not our only sources of counsel. We also find Kabbalistic teachings that speak to the needs and spirit of our time in much more mystical ways. One such teaching, from the Hasidic master Rabbi Abraham Joshua Heschel of Apt (1745–1825), hints at a broader definition of life than we often allow.

We are told in Leviticus 7:10–11 that Moses was instructed to anoint with oil all the surfaces of the tabernacle, as well as the holy vessels within it. Now, oil is linked in our sources with the quality of *chokhmah,* wisdom. Kings were anointed by pouring oil on their heads, the seat of wisdom: "You have anointed my head with oil," as David sings in the Twenty-third Psalm. "Let oil not be missing on your head," says Ecclesiastes 9:8. "There is treasure to be desired, and oil, in the dwelling of the wise," says Proverbs 21:20.

Wisdom, in turn, is closely associated with life: "Wisdom shall give life to those that have it" (Ecclesiastes 7:12). The well-known phrase that we recite when taking out the Torah on Shabbos, "*Etz chayim hi la-machazikim bah,* she is the Tree of Life to all who hold to her," is from Proverbs 3:18 and actually applies not to the Torah itself but to the universal quality of wisdom, the innate intelligence of our God-given soul.

What Moses was doing with the anointing oil, says Rabbi Heschel of Apt, was nothing less than bringing the sanctuary and its vessels to life. (What a wonderful stretch, to imagine a structure communicating with you like something alive and conscious. You walk in the door. You sense a greeting from the sanctuary itself: "Take off your shoes and come closer. Come with each step to a higher place, away from outerness, deeper into innerness, closer and closer to the Holy of Holies. Make room in your innermost heart of hearts. There will I be in my fullness.") What is the Apter saying? That if we look at something with *chokhmah,* with our deep intuitive wisdom, even the seemingly inanimate takes on a life and a holiness of its own. We see life where we saw none before.

To me, this kernel of Jewish insight, though expressed in long-defunct tabernacle imagery, speaks directly to one of the holiest ideas put forward by the scientific community in recent years: the idea that Earth itself is alive with a planetary intelligence of her own, innate, self-governing, self-sustaining, self-healing (see the "Window" box). Looking with wisdom at elements of creation that we previously considered inert, the proponents of the so-called Gaia hypothesis realized that we are part of a chain of life that extends all the way from the smallest drop of water to the largest weather system. Every part of that chain is integral to and necessary for life, from the atmosphere itself to the single-celled organisms that first shaped that atmosphere into a cradle for the continued unfolding of life. Every part is linked to every other in a vital, organismic relationship: without the microscopic mitochondria in my body's cells, for example, I couldn't exist, nor could they exist without me.

In the Gaia hypothesis, then, we see a *chokhmah,* an intuitive wisdom, that reveals life where we saw no life before. Seeing Earth as Gaia extends the "way of life"—the way that life accomplishes things: fluid, complex, interconnected, innately intelligent— higher than we have ever imagined. The hypothesis is controversial; scientists are still grappling with its implications. But I believe that the idea that the planet itself is alive holds out the possibility of renewing not only our scientific understanding, but the religious and spiritual lives of all those who live on our planet today.

## WINDOW: THE GAIA HYPOTHESIS

James Lovelock, who with macrobiologist Lynn Margulis was the author of the Gaia hypothesis, calls himself a geophysiologist. He was developing instruments for NASA to analyze the surfaces and atmospheres of other planets when he first became intrigued by the idea that the whole Earth—and not just its life-forms—was involved in sustaining itself. Lovelock doubted that NASA's efforts to detect life on Mars would bear fruit. The surest way to detect life, he thought, was not to grope around in the hope of finding life specimens, but to analyze the most easily available information about a planet: its atmosphere. Why? Because, just as we breathe out carbon dioxide, life-forms on other planets, too, would need to use the fluid mediums of atmosphere and oceans to deposit and carry away the products of their metabolism. This in turn would make the atmosphere recognizably different from the atmosphere of a dead planet.

Life is a very highly organized form of being, which is why it is so rare. As thermodynamics points out, the universe as a whole inexorably degenerates toward disorder. From a thermodynamic point of view, as Lovelock writes, life is "characterized by an omnipresence of improbability that would make winning a sweepstake every day for a year seem trivial by comparison."

Not only is life rare; so are the conditions necessary to sustain it. Life as we know it, at least, requires a nice comfy temperature, close to neutral pH, and an ideal concentration of various elements. What made us so lucky? The scientific community generally assumed that we had sprung up on such a hospitable planet by the luck of the draw—something to do with our ideal distance from the sun. Not so, said Lovelock and Margulis. Our distance from the sun was important, of course, but it was far from sufficient. Earth's current atmosphere sustains such an unlikely combination of gases, in chemical terms, that it requires a constant rebalancing of those gases and thus a great deal of energy directed to sustain it.

What provides this balance? Life itself. First came the photosynthesizers, the "producers" who convert the sun's energy into usable form and produce oxygen, among other things. Then came life-forms that, like ourselves, consume the photosynthesizers. We also breathe in the oxygen and restore carbon dioxide to the atmosphere—thus preventing an ultimately destructive buildup of photosynthetic products. Between them, producers and consumers built and preserve our atmosphere's crucial balance of oxygen, carbon dioxide, and other gases. Without the constant input of Earth's organisms, our atmosphere would quickly approach that of our dead neighbors, Mars and Venus: no oxygen, very little nitrogen, 98 percent carbon dioxide. Temperatures on Earth would rise to over 550 degrees Fahrenheit. No life could survive in such conditions.

For a planet to be as hospitable to life as ours is, the Gaia hypothesis states, life and the physical conditions necessary to support life—the atmosphere, oceans, climate, and crust—must have evolved together hand in hand, with each affecting the other, and must continue to sustain each other in the same tightly linked way. The Gaia hypothesis pulls Earth's inert ingredients into the cycle of life and points to a higher degree or scale of organization than we'd previously thought: an entire planet, not conscious as we think of the term, but alive with its own self-governing intelligence.

## GOD'S LIVING FACE

The images we use to explain our world to ourselves, though we are not always conscious of them, profoundly shape our

understanding. When Sigmund Freud was growing up, for example, the industrial world was powered by steam: steamships,
steam engines, factories driven by steam. So Freud imagined us
as all hot and steamy, full of libido. What will we do with all this
pressure? Will we suppress it, repress it, sublimate it, bleed off the
pressure in our dreams? It was a very mechanistic understanding—
and it revolutionized our image of our own psyches. Now imagine instead that Freud had grown up in the age of computers,
surrounded by terms like World Wide Web, parallel processing,
networks, servers, resident memory, clock speed, defragmenta-
tion, and core dumps. You can see how the path we've taken
toward psychological self-knowledge may have been different.

Let's take a look at how a more organic view of our world
might help give our tradition new meaning, starting with a central feature of traditional Jewish life. Almost every classic Jewish
blessing contains the phrase *melekh ha-olam,* king of the world.
Blessings have been central to the way we have related to God
for millennia, but today that phrase irks us. The word *king,* the
idea of a ruler—male, dominant, eternally "other"—no longer
makes sense to us. I believe, though, that this expression can take
on new meaning—if we shift the fundamental view of reality that
underlies it.

We have already seen in chapter 1 what power the word *king*
held for those who lived long ago. Society then was rigidly hierarchical in ways we can barely imagine today. Most people accepted without question their place in what leading thinkers told
them was a Great Chain of Being. The Chain of Being, they
believed, extended upward from the inanimate world through the
plant and animal kingdoms. Then came humans, from the lowli-

est up through the feudal order. Most exalted of all humans was the king or queen, upon whom rested the fate of his or her subjects. Above the sovereign, the heavenly spheres—uncorrupted, unlike the earthly sphere—had their own ascending order of royalty, from the lowlier angels that still maintained some connection to humankind and up through higher and higher heavenly beings until the throne of God himself, *melekh ha-olam,* king of the universe.

The idea of a Great Chain of Being was central to our understanding of the world around us from the time of Aristotle, all through the feudal Middle Ages, and on to the rigidly class-oriented societies of the late eighteenth century. It was a metaphor with tremendous power, girding up the very structure of society for centuries.

But today this view of reality no longer makes sense to us. Today we don't crown rulers: we vote for them. Men born in poverty have grown up to be presidents. Though women or non-Christians have yet to govern our country, we define no person as inherently better or more exalted than another. Kingdoms and feudal hierarchies have given way to states and corporations. These, too, are hierarchical, but the hierarchies are fluid. Science, once satisfied to study linear, often greatly simplified systems, is more and more interested in models that more closely approximate the complexity of *life:* chaos theory, complexity theory, information theory. The latest theories of business management, too, advise allowing productivity and creativity to emerge organically from within organizations. Slowly but surely, we are replacing the hierarchical Great Chain of Being as our core model for understanding our world with a Great Chain of Life, one that enfolds everything from the microorganisms that keep our planet alive to the planetary intelligence of which they are a part. (The "Chain of Life" is another hint from our tradition, an expression that already exists in the Jewish liturgy. In the Yizkor and memorial services, we pray that God will add the souls of our departed loved one to the *tz'ror ha-chayim,* the chain of life. Despite its association with mourning, it is not a morbid phrase but a hopeful one. May we live to see its significance greatly expanded in our day.)

Metaphors are so important. The more abstract the truth we are trying to grasp, the more we must rely on our imaginations—our human capacity to create images—to understand it. Nowhere has this been more true than in our visions of God, for if the world's religions agree on one thing, it is that the infinite God is beyond our power to grasp. The Kabbalists, for example, were especially perplexed by the question of how the infinite becomes finite—of how creation leaped that seemingly insurmountable barrier, and how we finite beings might somehow reconnect to the infinite. They came up with many complex and beautiful metaphors. Some imagined the existence of worlds upon worlds, parallel worlds in which the divine became ever more concretely manifest. Some spoke of *sefirot,* spheres or aspects of God, interwoven in a Tree of Life that was rooted on the earthly plane and had its crown in the heavens. Some spoke of *partzufim,* literally masks or faces, core images or names of God that embodied male and female, age and youth. In each case they were looking for an interface, a means to connect with the infinite, which would otherwise be so utterly beyond us.

I believe that Gaia, the face of our living planet, represents a newly emerging *partzuf,* or face of the ultimate core reality of the universe. What happens if we reimagine *melekh ha-olam* as the governing organismic wisdom of *ha-olam*—that is, of the planet Earth? All of a sudden we see phrases like "God is kind" or "God is merciful" in a new light. Instead of seeing God as an all-powerful patriarch in the sky, we can affirm that, yes, the universe is kind in the sense of being hospitable to life. Yes, the universe is compassionate in the sense that Earth heals her children. In our new understanding, such phrases become metaphors for the essential qualities of this planetary miracle we call life.

Does this mean that we replace the unknowable God with the name and face of Gaia, the Greek earth goddess? No. The God that I can know as an object of my mind is not God. The second commandment teaches us that every form or notion I have of God is an idol. But as our Sages said, the Torah speaks to us in human language. *Partzufim* are not God, but they help us connect. They help us charge up the God field, as it were. I don't always need to address God on a transgalactic scale. I can often be perfectly content to address the inherent intelligence of the universe as revealed right here on planet Earth.

## EARTHLY RESPONSIBILITIES

A more organic, rather than hierarchical, understanding can help us in other cases when the traditional religious worldview simply doesn't jibe with the world we know. The second paragraph of the *Shema,* for example, explains the success or failure of crops as God's will. In the old translations it sounded like this:

And if you will hearken diligently unto my commands which I command you this day . . . I will give rain of your land in its due season, the first rain and the last rain, that thou mayest gather in thy corn, and thy wine, and thine oil. And I will send grass in thy fields for thy cattle, that thou mayest eat and be full. Take heed to yourselves, that your heart be not deceived, and ye turn aside, and serve other gods, and worship them; for then the Lord's wrath be kindled against you, and he shut up the heaven, that there be no rain, and that the land yield not her fruit, and ye perish quickly from the good land which the Lord giveth you. (Deuteronomy 11:13–17)

This creates a problem for us. It just doesn't square with what we consider common sense, with what we feel in our hearts to be true. Today we don't turn to a rabbi or prophet to explain the weather: we ask a meteorologist. What our ancestors were doing, we would say, was mapping a divine system of reward and punishment onto natural—and therefore value-neutral—events.

Rabbi Lawrence Kushner discussed this passage once when I was visiting his shul in Sudbury, Massachusetts. He suggested that instead of reading this as materialist reward and vindictive punishment, we read it as karma, the inevitable results of the actions and choices we make in response to our planetary responsibilities. We note that the language here is not aimed at the individual, as so many of the mitzvot in Torah are, but at the group. As an individual I may not suffer as a result of environmentally harmful behavior, but as a cell in the group organism, I contribute to the group suffering somewhere down the line. Such thinking casts the passage in a new light. In an age of global responsibility, we need daily reminders. The Reconstructionist movement, which deleted this passage from the *Shema* in their early siddurs, are now bringing it back because they find it speaks so strongly to ecological concerns.

Today I prefer to render this and the following passages from the *Shema* like this:

*How good it will be when you really listen and hear my directions, which I give*
　　*you today,*
*for loving Yah who is your God,*
*and for acting Godly, with feeling and inspiration.*
*Your earthly needs will be met at the right time, appropriate to the season.*
*You will reap what you planted, for your delight and health.*
*Also your animals will have ample feed. All of you will eat and be content.*

*But be careful—watch out!*
*Don't let your cravings delude you.*
*Don't become alienated.*
*Don't let your cravings become your gods; don't debase yourself to them.*
*Because the God-sense within you will become distorted.*
*Heaven will be shut to you. Grace will not descend.*
*Earth will not yield her produce.*
*Your rushing will destroy you,*
*and Earth will not be able to recover her good balance*
*in which God's gifts manifest.*

*May these values of mine reside in your feelings and aspiration,*
*marking what you produce, guiding what you perceive.*
*Teach them to your children so that they are guided by them*

*in how to make their home sacred and how to deal with traffic!*
*May these values of mine reside in your feeling and aspirations*
*even when you're depressed or when you're elated.*
*Mark your entrances and exits with them, so you will be more aware.*
*Then you and your children and their children*
*will live out on earth that divine promise given to your ancestors:*
*to live heavenly days right here on this earth.*

# TRANSGRESSION

Today we are uncomfortable with the notion of sin or even, as Judaism prefers to think about it, transgression. Though some acts clearly seem good and others bad, the idea that some parts of our personalities should be stamped out so we can better conform to an exacting, divinely imposed code of behavior is one we find hard to accept. But in the Chain of Life nothing is truly garbage; nothing is thrown away. One cycle's waste becomes another's food. The God that is nature takes away from one life cycle and gives to another. The lotus, as the Buddhists say, grows in manure. Our job is to enlist in that process as much as we can, to ensure that the by-products of our existence are biodegradable.

How can the great metaphor of life bring us to a new understanding of transgression and repentance?

Imagine that you join a group of fellow Jews on the afternoon of Rosh ha-Shanah for the ceremony of *Tashlikh,* or "casting away." On this first day of the period of repentance that culminates with Yom Kippur, the Day of Atonement, we go to a body of water to cast away our sins. From an eco-kosher point of view, however, throwing away no longer makes sense. Now we realize that we cannot throw anything away—that there is no "away." Instead, what we cast out needs to be made biodegradable so that it can be recycled without causing additional pollution.

In order to connect to this process, we must realize how the behavior that we are attempting to throw away once helped to sustain us, and how it might help to sustain others somewhere down the line. In moving beyond what we now recognize as harmful behavior, we need to ask: "What did I learn? How did this behavior serve me?"

Suppose that I've been overeating. I know that this violates the halakhic injunction that we take care of our bodies, and I want to repent, to do *t'shuvah* on that. I make up my mind to stop. But it doesn't work: I continue to overeat. Why? Because I treat the overeating as my enemy. I need to remember that originally it came in as a friend. At one point it was necessary in my life— if I hadn't stored up when I did, perhaps I wouldn't have managed to live through a time that was lean in other ways, if not physically, then emotionally and spiritually.

Each quality, even those that seem bad, contributed somehow to our self-preservation. It had a good life-affirming purpose at one point, even if that is now no longer true. In order to let go of such a habit, I need to give it a "testimonial," to send it away with my thanks. "I needed you, and there you were, and I thank you for it. And now, with full appreciation, I know that I no longer need you and I can send you away." This is different from trying to stamp it out. We no longer say, "I'm sorry I did this. I'm throwing that behavior away." We say, "Thank you, God, for this gift. I needed it then; I no longer need it now. I am returning it to the universe in the hope that it can help generate life elsewhere as it did for me." And this needs to be true for all the things we want to say good-bye to at *Tashlikh*. This is what we mean by biodegradable.

## RESURRECTION

Another example of how an organic understanding can give new life to old ideas: Every time I recite the *Amidah* I thank God for reviving the dead. *T'chiyat ha-metim,* the resurrection or "enlivening" of the dead at the end of days, is the last of Maimonides' Thirteen Principles of Faith. *Yigdal,* the well-known morning prayer that casts the Principles in poetic language, closes with this thought. But how can I really affirm such a thing? I do not believe that graves will open up in cemeteries and corpses will crawl out of them. Should I believe that at some time at the end of days the individual cells of my remains will be reconstituted? Our bodies keep on changing. Every day we slough off old cells and grow new ones. How many bodies have I worn out already? Which of my bodies would rise at the time of the resurrection? How can I believe in the physical resurrection of the dead and mean it?

On the other hand, if I could only see myself for a moment as the planet sees me: welcoming me in 1924 and saying good-bye to me sometime in the future, being just one of the cells that has carried on its work. Then I could feel that, yes, this particular cell will someday die, but now it knows itself to be part of this vast living whole. When we see in our planet's life system a new face of God, we quickly find ways in which nonlife is coming alive all around us. Individual atoms may not be alive as we normally think of the term, but when atoms join together into molecules, molecules into organelles, and organelles into cells, then the lifeless comes alive. When you think of the information encoded in the chain of molecules that forms our DNA and RNA, the process by which the molecular ABCs get chained together into the literature of life is truly a miraculous enlivening, a *t'chiyat ha-metim*.

## A GAIAN *YONTIF*

We have already seen how a Shabbos practice connects us to a way of life more in tune with the cycles of nature. The same is true for the Jewish calendar as a whole, which, alone among those of the other great world faiths, is influenced by both sun and moon. The Jewish day ends and begins anew with the setting of the sun. Our months begin with the new moon. Many of our holidays fall on the full moon, the fifteenth day of the lunar month. We celebrate two of our most important holidays when the lengths of day and night are most closely balanced: Passover on the full moon closest to the vernal equinox, which marks the first day of spring, and Sukkot (the Feast of Tabernacles) on the full moon closest to the autumnal equinox.

Judaism also has a holiday specifically dedicated to nature: the New Year of the Trees, or Tu bi-Sh'vat, as the date is known, the fifteenth of the month of Shevat. It is well suited to emerge as a holiday of the future, a Gaian *yontif* (*yom tov* in Hebrew) or holiday, for two reasons. First, its significance has already changed several times over our history; and second, it is one of the few holidays that is celebrated with equal enthusiasm by religious and secular Jews alike.

Tu bi-Sh'vat is not mentioned in the Torah, which may be the secret to its flexibility. It makes its first appearance in the Mishnah, where the sage Hillel gave that date as the end of the "tax year" for the yearly tithes of fruit that Israelites brought to the priests and Levites and the poor.

The taking of tithes ended when the Temple was destroyed and the Jewish people went into exile. In the Diaspora, Tu bi-Sh'vat became a holiday where we ate fruits from the seven *minim,* or species of Israel (Deuteronomy 8:8), including grapes, figs, and pomegranates. The fruit reminded us of our homeland and sweetened our bitter exile. Besides the traditional blessing over fruit, however, the holiday had little or no liturgical content.

The Kabbalists who gathered in Safed in the wake of the expulsion from Spain gave Tu bi-Sh'vat new meaning and ritual. To them the holiday represented a turning from the darkness of winter to the light of spring and from the darkness of exile to the light of redemption. So they created a Tu bi-Sh'vat Seder to parallel the one on Pesach. They read passages relating to fruit from the Torah, the Talmud, and the mystical *Zohar;* recited blessings over fruit and flowering trees; and, as on Pesach, drank four cups of wine, each highly symbolic and accompanied by particular fruits.

Tu bi-Sh'vat acquired yet another face when trees became crucial to the Zionist dream of draining Palestine's swamps and making her deserts bloom. Thousands of Israeli children celebrated the day by going out to the countryside to plant saplings, while children in the Diaspora put coins in the light blue boxes of the Keren Kayemet (Jewish National Fund) to support their efforts.

All of these themes appear in the different celebrations of Tu bi-Sh'vat today. Traditional Jews remember its ritual significance. More environmentally minded Jews have given the holiday new life as a Jewish Earth Day, often combined with a Tu bi-Sh'vat Seder. The children in Israel plant trees.

Trees are clearly deeply significant to Jews. God's first act in the Eden story was to plant the trees of the Garden, and the trees of Life and of Knowledge represent the earliest and deepest part of our mythic consciousness. When Adam was first created, a midrash in Ecclesiastes Rabbah tells us, God led the first human around and showed him all the trees in the Garden of Eden. "Behold my works, how beautiful and commendable they are!" God told him. "I have created all this for you. Do not corrupt and destroy my universe, for if you do, there is no one to set it right after you."

The Mishnaic sages, the Kabbalists, the Zionists, and today's Jewish environmentalists—these and more have taken their turn at the growing edge of the Jewish tree. Maybe because of ancient Jewish antipathy toward pagan tree-worship, the mostly secular Zionists were the first to celebrate the whole tree and all trees, rather than just the edible fruit of fruit-bearing trees. In our day, when we clearly need trees to absorb carbon dioxide and to give us the essential fruit of oxygen, we should regard every tree as a fruit tree. In a truly Gaian holiday, we will celebrate them all.

# WAYS OF THE LIVING GOD

Once, the Talmud tells us, the scholarly houses of Hillel and Shammai were locked in a dispute about the law in a particular case. For three long years the dispute went on, until finally a voice from heaven intervened. *"Eilu ve-eilu divrei Elohim chayim,* these and these are the words of the living God." The voice went on to rule in favor of Hillel, but the initial statement speaks directly to the heart of an organic view of the world. Looking at this aphorism through the eyes of nature, we might reinterpret it to mean, "The attitude that 'These and these are the words of God'—this is *chayim,* life." This is the way God/Life operates. The organic model is not either/or; it is both/and. Life survives in the proliferation of possibilities, of viewpoints.

Religion and spirituality have too often been at war with science and modernity, but these and these are the diverse expressions of a living God. Each needs the other. A religion that stands only as the champion of the past will sooner or later cease to speak to us. But science needs spirit as well. Our faith connects us to the unknowable mystery that will always be at the heart of the scientific endeavor. We need the deep wisdom of the ancients to comfort and inspire us as we grapple with issues that are new and potentially very frightening. A science without both love and reverence is a cold endeavor indeed—and potentially dangerous as well. Finally, leaps of faith and intuition can take us to places where science cannot yet go.

Earth needs our help. The problem is that if we wait until

science establishes beyond doubt that our planet is sick, it may be too late. Of course we need the facts, but the facts are not calling us quickly and strongly enough to the service of a whole and healthy Earth. A scientist will spend decades studying the causes and effects of global deforestation. A mystic can listen with the inner ears of *chokhmah* and hear the scream of a troubled planet.

We need a new *partzuf,* or face of God, a vital mythology, that will keep our deepest intuitions alive. In every age and place, people have dreamed these mythic icons, and from them in turn emerged the legends, stories, meanings, motivations, and covenants of the age. Reshaping the *partzufim*—the faces, masks, inner templates that govern manifestation on this plane—is very deep and important work. The old imagery, the old language, so rigidly authoritarian and hierarchical, threatens to stifle us. We need the invigorating breath of fresh air that the *tz'ror ha-chayim,* the Great Chain of Life, can give us.

A vision of Earth that respects but transcends national and religious boundaries is part of the Torah of the future. We humans have the potential to be the global consciousness of a living planet, with every individual a conscious cell and every group a contributing organ of that *melekh ha-olam,* that vast living being. Gaia has already seen herself through our eyes: she'd been waiting so long to see her own *punim,* her own face! Now we have a choice: we can act like cancer cells, rogue cells sowing the seeds of the organism's destruction, or we can become Gaia's most flexible digits for healing herself where she hurts.

As creators of mythology for the future, we can opt for a Gaian understanding even if the facts have not yet forced us into it. We

can crown Earth's life-giving, life-sustaining intelligence as our
*melekh ha-olam,* our world-governing face of God. We can
broaden and refocus our *avodat ha-Shem,* our service to God, to
embrace service to the planet. We can reinterpret cosmic Kabbalistic phrases like *sh'virat ha-keilim,* the shattering of vessels,
and *tikkun olam,* the repairing of the world, to apply to the very
real Earthly possibilities of destruction and repair. We can remember the instruction in Proverbs 3:6, "Know God in ALL
your ways," seeing each and every action in the context of its
global significance. We can envision the future of human spirituality in harmony with our Gaian understanding. We can develop liturgies that will connect us—as individuals and peoples
alike—to the greater whole that is the life of Earth.

## CHAPTER 6

# WHY BE JEWISH?

BEING JEWISH in our culture is like swimming up-
stream. You're fighting the constant pull of other
commitments, fighting against your kids' resistance
to Hebrew school, fighting against the all-pervasive Christmas
season, and struggling to budget in those synagogue dues or to
choose a synagogue in the first place. Sooner or later—no matter how spiritual we are, no matter how connected we feel, deep
down, to our Jewishness—the question comes up: Why am I
doing this? Why be Jewish at all? Why hold on to this? Why pass
it on? What if I *were* the "last link in the chain"—would that
really be such a terrible thing?

In the ceremony of Havdalah, as we say good-bye to the
Sabbath and start our workweek, we bless the God "who sepa-
rates Israel from the nations." Why have we always insisted on
separating ourselves in this way? The taxes on being Jewish have

been so high: our history is littered with persecutions, pogroms, hounding and humiliation of every kind and on every scale. What for? Why perpetuate this cycle of violence? Was it worth it for my ancestors to endure so much just so I might be able to say "Mazel tov"? What is so great, so necessary, about Judaism? As a religion, we cannot claim to have the highest religious philosophy, to be the greatest artists of love and awe before God, or that our spiritual technology is the greatest or our liturgy the most beautiful. And haven't we gotten past the need for these Old World religions now? Aren't all religions talking about the same thing?

Why, then, is our way worth preserving? For whose sake am I doing this—for myself? My children? The Jewish people? God?

## MESSAGE FROM DHARAMSALA

In 1989, the Dalai Lama, leader of the Tibetan people in exile, appealed to the Jews for help. For fourteen centuries, Tibetan Buddhism had developed and flourished in a land surrounded on three sides by almost impassable mountain ranges, remote from the centers of power in India, Russia, and China. Then his people suffered a catastrophe that threatened to destroy them. Forty years had passed since the Chinese Army invaded Tibet, thirty since the Dalai Lama himself went into exile. Thousands of Buddhist monasteries and temples had been destroyed or desecrated. Monks and nuns were being imprisoned and tortured. More than a million Tibetans had died. In that same year, 1989, the Dalai Lama was awarded a Nobel Peace Prize for his nonviolent resistance of the Chinese occupation. But his people were faced with spiritual annihilation. They were scattered around the world, not only robbed of their land, their temples, their teachers, their traditional ways of life, but now subject to the relentless pressures of modernism as well.

Unfortunately, this scenario was familiar to us, for it was eerily similar to the fate the Jewish people had suffered at the hands of the Romans two thousand years before: our Temple destroyed, our people slaughtered, our teachers killed or silenced. "After we came to India," the Dalai Lama told author Rodger Kamenetz in *Stalking Elijah,*

> we learned how the Jewish community, the Jewish people, carried the struggle in different parts of the world and under difficult circumstances through such a long period; then we were very much affected. In the early sixties we often used to mention how we have to learn some of the Jewish secrets to preserve your identity and your culture and to develop it—in some cases, in hostile surroundings—over the centuries.

The Dalai Lama's question to the Jews was simple. "Tell me your secret," he said, "the secret of Jewish spiritual survival in exile."

It was also unprecedented. Here was the head of a world religion turning to the teachers of another faith and saying, in effect, "We find ourselves in a situation about which we have no knowledge. We need to learn how to transform our faith so that it might grow again from the ashes of our destruction. We need to reshape our faith to survive without a homeland. You, the Jews, are experts in this. Please help us. Please teach us." And so a delegation of us went to Dharamsala, India, the Dalai Lama's home in exile, to consult with His Holiness on how he might keep his people's spiritual heritage alive in a diaspora that still has no end in sight. The full story cannot be told here: Kamenetz devoted his book *The Jew in the Lotus* to our dialogue, and the conversation between our people is still ongoing. I emphasized the importance of parent-to-child transmission through tools like the Jewish Seder. Jews and Tibetans went on to celebrate Seders together—one of our most potent teaching tools—with the Tibetans saying "Next year in Lhasa"—their own Jerusalem, the capital of Tibet.

The Dalai Lama's plea to the Jews reversed the usual position that world faiths—including our own—take toward one another. Most Jews in Orthodox communities, for example, still hold on to a triumphalist vision of Judaism. Their thinking goes like this: "When the end of days will come, the Messiah will show that they were in error and we were free of error all along; we alone were right, and all the others were wrong." This is the Jewish version, but it sounds the same in the Vatican, in Mecca and Medina, and in hard-line communities everywhere:

"When the Second Coming is here . . ."

"When the Mahdi, the final Imam, appears . . ."

"When the last Hindu avatar arrives . . ."

That's the basic attitude of triumphalism: In the end it will be shown that *we* were the true carriers of the divine transmission and that all the others had failed. I call this the hydraulic effect: each is trying to push down the other in order to get themselves higher. Our tradition censures someone who does this as *ha-mitkabed be-kalon chavero,* one who aggrandizes himself at the expense of his fellow. Of course the concept of *chaver,* fellow or friend, does not extend to *goyim,* to the other. But it's hard to draw boundaries around a triumphalist attitude: it infects our thinking at every level. I grew up in the Hasidic community, among the Lubavitchers. In the early days of Hasidism, the disciples of the Baal Shem Tov would reach a certain level of spiritual attainment with one rebbe, then continue their study with another. Reb Schneur Zalman, the first Lubavitcher Rebbe, learned from the Maggid of Mezeritch, but he also learned from Reb Mikhal of Zlotchev and from Reb Pinchas of Koretz. In my day, though, the Belzer Hasidim would say, "None are truly for God except Belz," and the Lubavitch thought the same of themselves. Each Hasid seemed to march to the slogan of "One God, one Rebbe, one wife." Each sect adopted a uniform: to this day, you can tell which rebbe a man follows by the width of his hat brim or the color of his socks. "The army of God," the Lubavitch called themselves. Soon enough, though, splits appeared within their ranks: today the Lubavitch are divided into the "*meshichistim,*" those who believe that the last Rebbe was the *Mashiach,* the Messiah, and the "anti-*meshichistim.*"

If we think of the world as an organism, then triumphalism is a cancerous attitude. The cells of triumphalist organs want to go wild; they want to spread themselves so much that they will consume all the other cells in order to glorify that which is *them.* This is clearly not the way to go.

We who do not share this hard-line thinking sometimes go to the other extreme in coexisting with other faiths: "We are living in the modern world. We are all one global community now. We no longer want to see the world in terms of *us* and *them.* Of course, we need a little spice to life, so we'll keep our Hanukkah candles and they can keep their Christmas trees. But please, let's get rid of all the archaic stuff that has kept us fighting for so many centuries in the name of religion." This is clearly a more peaceful and benign way than the triumphalist attitude. Sometimes it's not even a belief we stand up and declare, but something we express by inaction, by staying away, by allowing our celebrations and rituals to slip away from our grasp.

But this, too, would homogenize the organism. To give up our own special way of being misses the mark. Certainly, we can make utopian statements that look forward to a future where religious and ethnic differences have been eradicated. But right now, I believe there is still a lot of mileage left in the contributions that we Jews—and other religions as well—have to offer to the world.

The Dalai Lama's vision was neither triumphalist nor what we might call homogenist, but organismic. What happens in a living being? The skin and the bones, the heart, brain, lungs, liver, and spleen all have different functions. Yet they are all connected. No life can survive if one of the vital organs was gone. Each organ needs to maintain its integrity in order to function. A person can live only because the liver is livering and the heart is hearting. We understand that instinctively. Our stubborn assertion of our individuality as a people, even here in America, is like a gland saying, "Don't you assimilate me. I need to do my work!"

When we look at our planet itself as an organism, we realize that every expression of diversity on this planet is part and parcel of Earth. At the highest level we are all one. But nowhere in nature do we find pure universalism: the universal always expresses itself in the particular. The nations and faiths of the world are the organs of this planet. And we as the Children of Israel have functions to carry out in this world for the benefit of the organism as a whole. That is why, having survived the persecution of two thousand years, we need to survive also the danger of dissolving into mere secularism or into a vaguely spiritual New Age soup in which the distinctive contributions of the various religions would be wiped out. That is why our instinctive reluctance to be the last link in the chain is a healthy one.

Different faiths, nations, and cultures perform a tremendous service to the planet in keeping their treasures alive. Think of a music like jazz. If jazz musicians in the New World had drawn only on the rhythms preserved in the courts of Europe, jazz would have been pretty tame stuff. Luckily, they still retained a sense of the complex, syncopated rhythms of Africa, the rhythm heart of the world. On the other hand, African music had little or no harmonic development: that's not what they put their resources into. For that, the jazz musicians turned to the traditions of Europe.

The mind-body-spirit revolution that has begun in the West shows us that the same is true regarding spiritual traditions. The Far East, for example, has kept martial arts alive for all of us; through their service the rest of us didn't need to become experts on how to use energy in that way. Similarly, though both Judaism and Christianity had their own rich traditions of meditation, these were known only to a very few. The world owes the East a debt of thanks for keeping this tradition alive for us, so that we can learn sitting from Zen and breathing and Yoga from India. On the other hand, the ancient and sheltered

traditions of Tibet had not evolved strategies for upholding a
spiritual tradition whose adherents were scattered around the
globe. The Dalai Lama knew nothing about maintaining a faith
through centuries of diaspora living. Thus he found himself
most urgently in need of Jewish expertise.

The Dalai Lama's extraordinary question shed new light on
what it means to be Jewish—or to be Christian, Muslim, Hindu,
or Buddhist. Why be Jewish? Because as Jews, we are stewards of
certain types of knowledge and experience that the world
needs. Of course, we are being Jewish for ourselves and our children, and for the Jewish faith, nation, and community as well,
but there's more to it than that. "Because of my love for *all* of
humankind, I want to be Jewish"—this is really the only answer
that can justify our stubborn refusal to cave in to the brutal pressures of history and the more subtle ones of the modern world.
This realization allows us to feel called not only by our past, but
by our present and future as well.

## WHAT WE BRING TO THE TABLE

To gain more confidence in our mission as Jews, we need to
gain a better understanding of two things. First, what are the
contributions that we Jews bring to the table? Second, why and
how does the world need what we have to offer? This understanding will help us be Jewish in a way that serves not only our
own spiritual needs and those of our families, but will help
maintain the health of the Jewish community as a whole and
contribute to the welfare of the planet.

We have already explored some of the particular strengths that Judaism has to offer for the benefit of the world.

First is our understanding of time. Modeling the practice of taking regular breaks from commodity time to reconnect with the cycles of nature is a tremendous contribution. That all humans benefit from a weekend is now well established, but the Jewish calendar offers us depths of meaning and holiness that no mere weekend can attain. Its power to anchor us in the natural cycles of days, moons/months, and seasons is extraordinary. Even a modest beginning is enough to start tapping into this. Try lighting candles with family and friends as the Friday evening sun goes down. Sing a song or two to welcome the Sabbath bride. Or invite your kids to watch the moon grow fuller and fuller as Passover approaches. "On the night of the full moon," you can tell them, "we will have our Seder." Older celebrants might be interested to know that the sun comes into this, too: the first nights of Passover and Sukkot (the Feast of Tabernacles) fall on the full moons closest to the spring and autumn equinoxes, respectively—the dates when the lengths of day and night most closely approach each other before starting to diverge again. These examples begin to give a sense of how our calendar links us to the cycles of moons and seasons. Unfortunately this treasure remains, for many of us, a largely untapped resource. I have a dream of seeing in my lifetime a retreat center or religious community where people would take it upon themselves to live the liturgical year fully and consciously. The more we immerse ourselves in these cycles, the more we experience the benefit of living in organic time.

The second Jewish idea that we discussed is kashrut. The

centuries-old distinction that our ancestors maintained between kosher and unkosher foods, even if we ourselves do not observe it, created in us a vigilance about what we put into our mouths that lasts to this day. Examining a label for fat or fiber content is an outgrowth of our tradition's insistence that we need to have kosher food. Our task now is to expand this discriminating awareness to encompass proper use of all our planet's resources. To remember that each thing consumed has an origin and a cost. To ask: How can I consume what I need for life while minimizing cruelty and waste in the world? How does this act of consumption affect me and my surroundings on *every* level, spiritual as well as physical? With such conscious acts we can begin to raise the act of consumption to a higher plane.

Another precious inheritance that Jews can share with the rest of the world is our approach to *talmud torah,* or study. The attraction that books and intellectual pursuits still have for many Jews today comes from generations upon generations of people for whom study was important, and who made sure to pass on their love of learning to their children. Jews have always had the idea that just as sheet music isn't music until it is played and heard, Torah isn't Torah until it is interacted with. In offering this tradition to the world, we can open up this definition of Torah to mean any text that lies at the heart of a culture, that serves as its blueprint and moral compass. For Jews this means Torah and Mishnah and Talmud and all of our sacred commentaries. For Americans this could apply equally well to the Declaration of Independence and the Constitution, the revelation that our founders received.

The idea that grappling with our sacred texts is the right and obligation of lay people as well as clergy is a Jewish idea. For his crime of daring to translate the Latin scripture into English vernacular in 1380, the Church dug up John Wyclif's bones and burned them. William Tyndale, whose translation was published in 1525, was strangled and burned at the stake. Jewish leaders, on the other hand, have been preoccupied with bringing Torah to the people since at least the time of Ezra. Our tradition made the study of Torah and Talmud part of the daily regimen of every Jew who could possibly manage it.

Talmud torah has always meant more than just reading. The blessing we say before studying thanks God for the commandment *la-asok be-divrei Torah,* to busy or engage ourselves in the words of Torah, to roll up our sleeves and get into it, to make it real. The traditional house of study was not a quiet and reverential place but a loud and vigorous free-for-all, as each pair—study traditionally took place in pairs—argued the point back and forth in an attempt to reach true understanding. The models for these discussions were the arguments between the sages in the Mishnah and the Talmud, in which the dissenting opinions were lovingly preserved along with those that finally won the day.

For this was never just abstract study. Conclusions had to be reached. In the final blessing before the *Shema* in the morning prayers we ask God to give our hearts the power "to learn and to teach, to keep and to perform all the words of your Torah's teachings—with love." Two points emerge here. The first is that Torah study always demands from us a "therefore," a conclusion, an action directive, a better understanding of the mitzvot we are to "keep and perform." We are not at liberty to leave what we learned in the study hall, but are commanded to take our conclusions out into the real world.

The second point is that we do not apply only cold intellect to our study, but heart as well, and a sense of joy. The Hasidic teacher Reb Abraham Joshua Heschel of Apt used to introduce his conclusions with the words *be-ha'ir lev ve-sum sekhel,* which roughly translates as "putting our hearts and minds to it." We operate not only with *sekhel,* with intelligence, but *be-ha'ir lev,* with the awakening of heart. Someone once asked me, "You Jews have a religion of *law.* We Christians have a religion of grace. Isn't it so?"

"Let me ask you a question," I replied. "Did you ever take a book of canon law and dance with it?"

"What do you mean?" he said. "Why would we do that?"

"Our Law is a law that we dance with," I told him. "We kiss it." Could you imagine being a Baptist who is coming to shul for the first time and sees the Torah being carried around, people kissing it? *Something* is going on! We study with both minds and hearts. The translation of *Torah* as "Law" doesn't capture it. The kind of engagement that we offer the world with the expression "Torah study" is a whole other thing.

In our daily and democratic grappling with our sacred texts we were never content to leave divine revelation up to heaven; Torah, for us, belongs here on earth. Unlike Islam, which comes from the word for surrender, Jews surrender nothing to God. Our ancestor Jacob received the name Israel because he wrestled with God (Genesis 32:28): that is what *yisra-el* means. The tradition of argument began with Jacob's grandfather Abraham, who greeted God's plans to destroy Sodom and Gomorrah with vigorous debate: "Come on. The Judge of the whole world won't do justice?" (Genesis 18:23–33). Abraham got God to agree to save the cities even if only fifty righteous men were found there—then argued God down to ten. "The defense attorney," Rashi calls him. Moses put his life on the line in similar circumstances: when God threatened to wipe out the entire people after the sin of the Golden Calf, Moses responded, "Wipe me, then, off the book you have inscribed" (Exodus 32:32), as if to say, "Don't you do that to me, Lord. I won't have any part of it."

It's easy to justify a status quo, unjust as it may be, as "God's will." That has never been the Jewish way. If an unjust status quo is God's will, then God must stand corrected! Our sources tell of how the Sages refused to accept even a voice from heaven as decisive in a matter of *halakhah*—and of God smiling, saying, "My children have bested me." The chutzpah of calling God onto the carpet as Abraham and Moses did—of advocating and haggling and conniving on creation's behalf—is something I haven't seen anywhere else.

A Hasidic teaching recommends that a person carry two pieces of paper in his pocket. One should say, "I am but dust and ashes." The other: "For me the world was created." We need each of these reminders at different points in our lives. The first phrase is one that Abraham used in defending Sodom and Gomorrah before God. We know how often the crusade on behalf of a righteous cause can lead us into arrogance. At that point we need the reminder that we ourselves are nothing special.

We also know how life can make us doubt our own self-worth, even to the point of wondering whether our continued existence is worth it. At that point we need the opposite perspective. *The entire world was created for me.* I may be one among billions, but my existence on this earth is necessary and precious. It is also a challenge. Creation and the gift of life have been handed to me personally. What can I do today to fulfill that trust? How will I respond to that responsibility?

And so Jews have never shirked from joining the struggle. The number of Jews who have devoted themselves to some form of *tikkun olam,* repair of the world, is something we can be proud of. But oy, the cost has been heavy sometimes. At one point in my life, I was trying very hard to understand why the Jews had to endure all the various sufferings that have befallen us in the world. I thought my chances might go up a little if I asked someone who really knew! So I turned my question over to God. An image came to me then of God sitting in heaven saying, "Whom shall I send? The hatred people harbor in their hearts for one another and the genius for destruction that they have are converging toward catastrophe. There is a terrible lesson here that the world must learn. Who will go for us?" And I had the sense that somewhere along the line we volunteered. We said, "Master of the Universe, if karma, the law of retribution in the cosmos, would have its way, the world would drown in its own dung. The world and all its life cannot exist without somebody serving as the cells that fight infection in the body of humanity. If you need someone to serve as an example, we will go." And so, like white corpuscles fighting infection, we died in our millions. Others nations, too, have served in this way: West Africans who died in slavery, Native Americans, Armenians, so many others. Who knows? Maybe it is the only way the human race can learn the lessons of racism, conquest, arrogance, hatred. We pray that such a terrible cost at least brought some benefit.

Over the course of many centuries, we Jews have learned how to deepen our faith and joy and connection to God in the midst of uncertainty, vulnerability, and powerlessness. Other faiths can offer the world their expertise in dealing with the challenges of aligning a religion with worldly power. Christianity is a prime example: the separation of church and state that we treasure in this country is a direct result of the Church's experiments with the alternative. Islam has not yet come to this conclusion. Our expertise as Jews is different. Until the establishment of the State of Israel, we were not distracted by the responsibility for running states and fielding armies. Living in exile freed us from the corruption of power and taught us to survive without its benefits. As the Dalai Lama recognized, we Jews had become specialists in the pursuit of a holiness that was both deeply rooted in this world and, at the same time, completely independent of worldly structures of power. If the phrase "a light unto the nations" has any justification, it is that for most of our life as a faith we did our mission not by coercion, but by modeling our convictions.

We are experts in exile. This wisdom is something we can offer people of all faiths, not just Tibetans, because in a sense we are all living in exile. Exile from truth, from certainty, from invulnerability is part of our condition as human beings, individually and as a race. We feel that every day. That is why Jews still look forward to the coming of the Messiah, and Christians to a Second Coming. We have not yet been redeemed. We still have no clear sense of what we need to do to ensure the greater health of our species and our planet as we go into the future.

The answer we have offered to "Why be Jewish?" then, is that Judaism has many deep teachings to offer that we still need today:

Judaism reminds us to recalibrate ourselves by nature's clock.

Judaism teaches us conscious consumption.

Judaism urges us to maintain a living dialogue with the texts that are the beating heart of our culture.

Judaism demands here-on-earth spirituality.

Judaism helps us maintain faith and a connection to God despite powerlessness and uncertainty.

These treasures are the birthright of each and every one of us. For all these reasons, we can be proud of our heritage and feel that it is still something that the world needs.


## "GETTING IT TOGETHER" TOGETHER


I believe, though, that as far as the planet is concerned, we've gone about as far as we can go as separate and isolated faiths. We are only just now reaching an understanding of the service that each tradition has performed for the world. We need to open up better channels of communication. God has given every faith some vitamins that the others need, and we won't be able to survive in health unless we exchange these vitamins. We need to start taking counsel with one another. We need to turn our spiritual software—the technologies of transformation that we have developed over the centuries—into shareware. The only way we can "get it together" is together.

The problem is that religions still don't have a way of regarding the "other" that makes sense as we go into the future. Each organ has built up its own immune system. We've been rejecting one another, and deadly infections keep breaking out. The Holocaust in Christian Europe amputated a third of the Jewish organ of the world. Six million cells were lost and priceless DNA as well. We may never replace the holy wisdom of Hasidic Europe, for example. We must replenish ourselves in other ways. But how can we retain our specificity and rebuild our spiritual strength and intensity without the fanaticism that has accompanied such intensity in the past?

We need a third way, one that neither takes a triumphalist stand nor demands a total lowering of the immune response and loss of specificity. We who are spiritually hungry sometimes feel a closer kinship with like minds from other faiths than with co-religionists who seem to be operating on automatic. This opens up what I call a dialogue of devoutness: a comparing of notes by those who revere and love God, a sharing of insight and understanding. The Dalai Lama initiated such a dialogue when he turned to the Jewish people for help. Wherever searching spirits encounter one another today, whether in a formal dialogue or in an interfaith family or group holiday celebration, the dialogue continues.

Today we see more and more committed, searching, alive souls, no matter what lineage or tradition they are from, who have a bit of a hyphen in their identity. The Trappist monk and widely published author Thomas Merton was one such person. Merton needed some Zen and some Taoism for his soul's well-being. Catholicism, with all of its vast magisterium, its transcendental appeal, even with its history of true mystics like Meister Eckhart and others, wasn't enough for him without the wisdom of Lao-tzu, the Chinese sage. This same hyphenated consciousness is what made Father J. M. Dechanet, a Benedictine monk, write a book like *Christian Yoga* (1960), or Father William Johnston, a Jesuit priest, write *Christian Zen* (1971). It is the same multilayered consciousness that fills the zendos and ashrams with "Jew-Bus" and "Hin-Jews."

This hyphenation tells us that our spiritual hunger has a universal component in it that will not be satisfied only by what one tradition produces by itself, for itself. The whole truth? Who knows the whole truth? The truth that any one religion has glimpsed can only be a partial truth. Anyone who seeks to make a genuine spiritual connection today needs to hear the witness that comes from other sides.

In a dialogue of the devout we speak as practitioners of separate paths who all seek to stand in the presence of God. We are not looking for a theological argument. Rather, we are looking over the fence at the means that other faiths use for spiritual transformation. So we come to dialogue not to whittle down our differences, but to maximize the connection we feel to the universal presence in the universe. Fundamentalists feel that admitting that another faith may have a contribution to make will weaken your belief in your own faith. I don't buy that: I think soul knowledge knows how to go outside the box. To me, it works the other way. One searching soul recognizes another— far out! "Oy, you also love God. What a wonderful thing this is."

Spiritual seekers need one another as mirrors. A member of

the Hopi nation once asked me about our holy days. I was telling him about Passover, our celebration of freedom, and Sukkot, our Feast of Tabernacles, and how they fit in with the cycles of the year. "I think I get it," he said finally. "You people don't want to be in slavery. You want to be free. And you want to pass this on to your children. But when you tell your kids on Passover, 'We have to go away from here; we can't stay here because it will cost us our freedom,' your kids will say, 'Yeah, but what are we going to eat?' So you teach them how to bake bread on stones, how to roast a lamb if you are hungry, how to find dandelion greens, and so on. When the kids ask, 'But where are we going to stay?' you show them how to build a lean-to, so they will have somewhere to live." An Indian perspective on the mitzvot to eat the Passover lamb with matzot and bitter herbs and to build a sukkah on Sukkot gave me a completely different insight into my own tradition.

## FROM INNER FAITH TO INTERFAITH

How do we engage with fellow seekers in a way that does not water down differences, but treasures them? How do we share our history, celebrations, and spiritual experience with members of other faiths in a way that is real and deep, rather than just a "You bring the Easter eggs; I'll bring the matzah" affair? Many today no longer feel the suspicion and resentment that past generations felt toward the other. We can seize this opportunity to acknowledge our debts to one another and explore the richness of every faith's unique qualities.

## Judaism Before the Patriarchs

I want to begin by acknowledging our debt to the religions that surrounded us when Judaism first began. Pagans—what our sages called "worshippers of stars and signs"—stood very low in the traditional Jewish ranking of human beings, the seven Canaanite nations in particular. Only Amalek, our archetypal biblical oppressors, were lower. But what was paganism if not prepatriarchal Judaism? Abraham did not invent Judaism out of thin air. We know, for example, that Abraham, or Abram as he was then known, received some form of divine transmission through Malchizedek, a local king.

> And Malchizedek king of Salem brought forth bread and wine: and he was the priest of the most high God. And he blessed him, and said, Blessed be Abram of the most high God, possessor of heaven and earth. And blessed be the most high God, which hath delivered thine enemies into thy hand. And he gave him tithes of all. (Genesis 14:18–20)

*Malchi-tzedek* means righteous king. Salem, *Shalem* in Hebrew, means whole or at peace; the city that, by tradition, became Jeru-salem. What exactly was transmitted here we don't know, but I believe the teaching had something to do with the bread and wine that Malchizedek gave to Abraham. We note that he didn't give him grapes and wheat, but instead the result of what happens when those natural materials "spoil," or ferment, on this level in order to rise to the next, the level of sacrament.

We also note how the *partzuf,* or face of God, had evolved for Malchizedek at this point. Earlier forms included what the Torah calls a *matzeva:* a rock, a phallic sign. We know that some gods were given the faces of animals, zoomorphic forms like Anubis, Hathor, Sekhmet. After a while the gods were seen anthropomorphically. But Malchizedek, "priest of the most high God," had reached an entirely different level.

I believe our ancestors learned not only from Canaan but from Egypt, too, as they took the first steps on what would eventually be the Jewish path to God. Where did the practice of circumcision come from? The Assyrians and Canaanites didn't practice it: the Egyptians did. Why did God appear to Abraham in the plains of Mamre after Abraham was circumcised? Because, as even the great commentator Rashi admits, it was Mamre—or Mem-Ra, a good Egyptian name—who counseled Abraham to do it.

God sent us to Egypt not only to learn that "because we were slaves, we should be good to others," but also to experience the high culture that existed there. How else did a shepherd people begin the process of becoming refined enough to reach Sinai? I remember walking around in wonder in the Egyptian museum in Cairo and feeling, "*Barukh ha-Shem,* thank God that we were in Egypt to learn from such a high civilization." We have never acknowledged how much we owe Egypt for the teachings that Moses must have received in the court of Pharaoh. We have always stressed how bad the Egyptians were and acted as if Moses, our greatest leader, came from nowhere. But take a look: Moses was raised as a prince in Egypt. Wouldn't he have received the best education that anyone could get? He would have spent his formative years at the prep schools and Ivy Leagues of the ancient world.

Then, at the age of twenty, he runs away to the desert. And
what does he do there? Shepherds the flocks of Jethro, "priest of
Midian," and ultimately marries his daughter. When it comes
time for his father-in-law to say good-bye to the Children of Israel, Moses pleads with him to stay and be "their eyes" in the
desert (Numbers 10:31). Jethro refuses; he returns to his country
and his people. But we can see how young Moses, that extraordinary young man, having obtained a Ph.D. from the university,
then apprentices himself to the Beduin sheikh, keeper of desert
lore, like Carlos Castaneda and Don Juan. The high culture of
Egypt, the secrets of the desert, the patience and watchfulness of
the shepherd—all these must have been crucial in the formation
of the greatest prophet our people has never known.

The people we call pagans were stuttering to tell us something important. We rebelled against their notion of individual
gods, but the *partzufim* that they developed for the infinite tapped
into very deep currents in our psyches and souls. Some of our
most potent Jewish rituals draw much of their power precisely
from the vestiges they contain of the old nature-based religions.
That power, because it is so ancient, can transcend our more modern definitions of Jew, Christian, Muslim, Buddhist, and Hindu.

I experienced this in June 1992, when I was asked to join
over two dozen representatives of religious and spiritual traditions
from around the world who gathered in Rio de Janeiro, Brazil.
The purpose was to stage a "people's event" that would celebrate the sacredness of the earth in parallel to the "Earth Summit"
(United Nations Conference on Environment and Development).
I was asked to represent the Jewish take on ecology, but because
of the many traditions represented, we were each given six min-

utes to convey what we wanted to convey. Spending that six minutes talking would clearly have been a waste of time. I wanted to invite the crowd to a ritual that would go deeper than words. So I decided to expand on the ritual that we Jews perform on Sukkot, the Feast of Tabernacles—even though Sukkot was still over two months away.

The first day of Sukkot falls on the full moon of the autumnal equinox. In ancient Israel, during Temple times, Sukkot was the harvest festival and marked the traditional beginning of the all-important rainy season. Traditional Jews today still build sukkot, or temporary booths, as the Torah and rabbis instructed us to do, roofed over by what we would call agricultural waste— cornstalks now empty, palm fronds, bamboo stalks, and so on. We take our meals there; some people even sleep in the sukkah, in order to realize for themselves how much they are protected by the wings of the Divine Presence—for in Hebrew the word *sukkah* has the same numerical equivalent as the names YHVH and ADNI *(Adonai)*.

On Sukkot we celebrate the expressions of nature in the earth and in ourselves. "When you have gathered in the land's bounty, you shall celebrate a festival unto the Lord," Torah instructs us. "Take the fruit of goodly trees, branches of palm trees, boughs of leafy trees and willows of the brook, and rejoice before the Lord your God seven days" (Leviticus 23:40). Jewish tradition interprets these four species as the *lulav,* a long palm frond that is lashed together with shorter branches of the willow and the leafy myrtle tree. The "fruit of goodly trees," by tradition, is an *etrog,* or citron, a large citrus fruit. The long lulav wand, with its shorter companions on either side, clearly symbolizes the masculine, the heavy round etrog the feminine. During the ceremony of *Hosha'anot,* or supplications, we move the lulav and etrog in toward our hearts, then extend them outward, shaking them slowly to the four winds, then up, then down. We dedicate the masculine and feminine forces to God in this way. We pray that bountiful rains should come down, that the winds should blow and the air be purified. These prayers must have been particularly fervent in ancient times: without a good rainy season, the following year would be hungry and hard.

I could think of no better way of praying for the healing of the planet in Brazil than this ceremony of *Hosha'anot.* Since I couldn't find a myrtle tree or citron, I used another local plant and a large papaya. As I waited anxiously in the wings for my turn, I felt like a priest about to bless the people. I thought of calling on Aaron, the biblical priest, to take over in me, to gird me up. But Aaron, brother of Moses, wouldn't have done this, I felt. He would have been too Jewish for that. The people of the entire world were gathered here! And so the figure I prayed to take over in me instead was Malchizedek, the ancient king, priest to the most high God.

Finally it was my turn. "We are praying here for the health of the planet," I told the gathering, "for the rain and the wind and the air. We recite the traditional line, '*Ana ha-Shem, hoshi'a na*— Please, God, help us.' Please join me by reciting a similar line from your own tradition: Christians could say *kyrie eleison,* which means the same thing; Moslems could address Allah in their traditional way, *ya-rachman, ya-rachim;* Hindus could say *om shanti, shanti, shanti,* and so on." So we prayed in the four directions, then up for the ozone layer and down for the water table, waving the lulav and etrog three times in each direction. My Jewish colleagues followed each set of movements with a loud blast from the *shofarot,* or rams' horns.

When we finished, a great cry went up. People got it. These rituals, archaic and outmoded as they may seem—or perhaps *because* of those very qualities—are extremely powerful. Who among us has not been moved by a blast from the shofar, that most ancient of spiritual technologies? This ceremony had shown that these rituals could reach beyond the Jewish people, that they could reach out to an entire planet in quest of healing.

## The Rebbe of Nazareth

American and European Jews do not live surrounded by Canaanites, as our biblical ancestors did, but by Christians. Christians are our neighbors, friends, colleagues, and family members. We have people today who are saying, "I want to embrace Judaism, because my partner is a Jew and my children are part Jewish. I am married to this faith, and I want to have Jewish content in my life—but I also want to be able to go to church. I cannot turn my back on my Christian upbringing." In the past, we would have said the two are incompatible. But I want to create a compatibility because I feel that compatibility in my heart.

I needed to take some time out once and decided to spend a couple of weeks with the monks at the Benedictine Monastery in Snowmass, Colorado. Some of the men there were veterans in the dialogue of the devout, including Father Thomas Keating, a leading figure in introducing Christian contemplative practices to people of all denominations, and Father Theophane Boyd, founding elder of the Interfaith Peacemaker Order and a leader in Buddhist-Christian dialogue. I stood with them at Vespers, Vigils, Lauds, and the other canonical hours, reciting *tehillim* (psalms) in the back of the church while they sang in the choir at the center. When Friday came around, I spoke to some of the monks in the kitchen. "Shabbos is coming. Could I have some candles and grape juice and rolls?" They fixed me up, and we had a Friday night *tish,* the Hasidic term for a sacred gathering around the table. It was wonderful.

The following week they said, "Would you do that again?" Yes, I said—but let's do a little role-playing. I will be Joseph of Arimathea—the Jew who was "looking for the kingdom of God," as the Gospel of Mark describes him, and was enthralled by the teachings of Jesus. You be disciples of Jesus who come from Galilee to Jerusalem, and we'll have a Shabbos together as they had in those days. And so we did. I lit the candles and made kiddush. We sat around the table and sang songs from the Psalms that my old friend Rabbi Shlomo Carlebach had set to music, songs like "I lift up my eyes unto the mountains" and "For the love of my brothers and friends." Then I said, "Nu, what's the news from Galilee? What stories do you bring from the Master?" They got very excited about that, and each told a different story from the Gospels. Together, we found that by reaching back to our common past, we were able to create a compatibility and enrich one another spiritually.

Could Jews and Christians sit down to study together, as well? The words of Yeshua of Nazareth, after all, are the teachings of a rebbe to his Hasidim, all of whom lived and died as Jews. He meant them as a midrash, or commentary, on Torah. The Gospels

are therefore partly Jewish books. The point that we need to remember is that Jesus was a teacher of *aggadah,* not *halakhah*—a
teacher of mythic lore, not law. He taught, as the Hebrew phrase
gocs, *ke-echad ha-moshlim,* as one of the parable weavers, one who
speaks in similes. The Gospels attest to this in numerous places.
(See for example Matthew 13:10, 13:13, 22:1; Mark 3:23, 4:2,
4:33–34.) Aggadah takes us into a very different space than halakhah. In yeshiva, when we would encounter the aggadic bits
in the otherwise legalistic language of the Talmud, our teachers
switched the singsong in which they read to a minor key. The
switch signaled that this language was not to be taken as deno-
tative, that is, specific and explicit, but rather connotative, with
levels of meanings beyond the literal. We knew we were entering what for Judaism was a futuristic space, one associated with
the coming of the Messiah in the end of days.

I believe that the confusion between aggadah and halakhah
has brought some Christians great pain. When Jesus says, in the
Sermon on the Mount, "If thy right eye offend thee, pluck it
out and cast it from thee" (Matthew 5:29), not even the staunchest
fundamentalist would go to thc cyc doctor and say, "This eye has
offended me. I'd like to have it removed." Everybody understands that this statement is aggadic, not halakhic—a metaphor,
not a law. The same is true not only for "Whosoever looks on a
woman with lust has already committed adultery with her in his
heart" (Matthew 5:28)—clearly an aggadic statement—but also,
I believe, for a statement on marriage like "What God hath
joined together, let not man put asunder" (Matthew 19:6). By
taking this as law, rather than parable, Catholics have caused themselves no end of unhappiness. Taken as a halakhic statement, this

pronouncement is even harsher than the famously strict rabbinical House of Shammai, who said that at least in the case of adultery you can have a divorce, and people can start a new life. But
for Catholics their only recourse is the legal fictions couples
must resort to in order to have marriages annulled.

Studying this midrash with our Christian brothers and sisters
would not only help us to recover our part in it, but might help
Christians to understand it better as well. In Matthew 16:18-19,
for example, Jesus tells his disciple: You, Peter, are the rock upon
whom I will build my church. "I will give you the keys to the
kingdom of heaven. Whatever you bind on earth will be bound
in heaven, and whatever you loose on earth shall be loosed in
heaven." Most Christians have difficulty understanding this language. But more traditionally minded Jews would have no problem with it, since the standard Hebrew word *issur*—that is,
binding—means prohibition under Jewish law, while *heter*—or
loosening—refers to the declaration of an act as permitted. While
we do not accept Peter or the popes that followed him as the
source of halakhic decisions, sharing such sacred vocabulary with
our Christian friends would give a much clearer picture of what
Jesus meant.

Looking over the fence and seeing some of the beautiful ways
in which Christians have responded to the infinite can charge
up our own religious lives as well. We can read someone like
Thomas Merton; meditate on a phrase like Meister Eckhart's,
"The eye with which God sees you is the one with which you
see God"; listen to "Jesu, Joy of Man's Desiring" or any of the
other glorious liturgical music of Bach. Christmas, too, has

something to teach us. Every Christmas I get a real yearning for the Christian ability to imagine God as a baby. Seeing God as a newborn babe, you begin to see that even God needs to grow, just as we do! And that this may really be the purpose of the universe—that we ourselves are God growing Godself, and that the task of every person and faith community is to collaborate in that process.

Kneeling is a very special, very holy practice. Jews used to kneel more than they do today: bringing the practice back into Judaism would be a mitzvah. Remember the movie *Moonstruck?* Cher wants Danny Aiello to propose to her properly, so, in front of a whole restaurant, he gets down on his knees. His fellow Italians really dig the whole scene. But let's take a look at what's happening here. Getting on your knees in front of another is like saying, "Please, may it be your will. If you answer my entreaty, there will be a change in both of us. We will no longer be single individuals. We will be joined together." The same is true when we get on our knees before God. Praying from a standing position is almost like saying, "I and Thou, we are equals." Our minds are satisfied with this. But then comes a time that our hearts are really in anguish, and we find ourselves "standing in the need of prayer," as the old song goes. *Prayer* is from the Latin *precari,* to entreat. In a truly precarious and desperate situation, the heart might say to the mind, "Please. I need to entreat God on my knees about this."

Christians have taught me a thing or two about conducting a service, too. One morning I was supposed to give a talk at a Presbyterian church. I asked the minister if I could come for the service as well, and of course he welcomed me to do so. As part of the service he gave a sermon, but before he began, he turned to the congregation and said, "Please pray for me that I might be a vehicle for the word of God to you." Several moments passed in silence, and they all prayed for him; and then he began the sermon. How wonderful that was!

Another example. In our own synagogues we have what we call *birkat ha-gomel,* the prayer of thanksgiving. Between portions of the Torah reading, anyone can get up and say a brief blessing thanking God for healing them from an illness or for helping them survive some other dangerous situation. If you go to a Christian Science church, you'll find that they often do the same thing, but they really get into it. "I give testimony to the healing of the spirit in my life. I was suffering in such-and-such a way, and then I invited Christ into my life, and I was healed. And I appreciate the healing that God sent to me, and the messengers of healing"—and they might name the Christian Science practitioners who helped them. One after another they testify like this. It's very powerful.

Once we get this reminder and start looking around in our own sources, we quickly realize that we, too, used to take such occasions more seriously. The Talmud derives *birkat ha-gomel* from Psalm 107, which tells of those saved from hunger, storms, imprisonment, and death who "dedicated offerings of thanks, singing hymns to tell of God's deeds." In Temple times you would give a sacrifice, invite all your friends, tell them what you went through. Some communities today still have the custom of holding a feast of thanksgiving when one survives a life-threatening situation.

. . .

WHERE DO WE draw the line? How far is "too far" in sharing the rituals of other faiths? After all, we have a long history of very deep *tzores* with the Christians. The name of Jesus was greeted with great bitterness in Jewish Europe. We had suffered so much in his name. *Er farfiert die ganze Welt,* the Yiddish saying went: he seduced the whole world into believing in him. If a Jewish person goes to a Buddhist center or a Hindu ashram—Nu, the parents get upset, but it's not the end of the world. But let a Jew mention the name of Jesus and oy, oy, oy, everyone gets very excited.

That Christianity has inflicted much pain in the name of Jesus, there is no question. We of my generation, at least, cannot forget this. And yet we should remember that all those centuries of persecution started as a family quarrel, a struggle between older and younger siblings for the love of the Father. Just as ancient Jews defined their faith by drawing borders between their beliefs and practices and those of the pagan Canaanites around them, so did the early Church define itself vis-à-vis the Jews who did not accept the teachings of their rebbe.

Paul of Tarsus was a master at carving out this new Christian space. He argued and split hairs like a Lithuanian yeshiva *bocher.* What was Paul saying? We died in Christ (Galatians 2:20 and Colossians 3:3). What did this mean? His Jewish listeners would have understood that dead people don't have to do mitzvot. Traditionally, for example, when a person was buried, we would rip the tzitzit from the one of the corners of the tallis he was wrapped in, symbolizing the end of his obligation to perform the commandments. Certain orders of monks and nuns today still wear

a garment with a hood called a scapular: it's a four-cornered garment *without* tzitzit. This distinguished the followers of Jesus
from the rest of the Jewish community in the early development
of Christianity: if, so to speak, you saw a person wearing an un-
tzitzified garment, you'd know they were one of what we later
called the *toite hasidim,* followers of a dead rebbe. So we didn't
buy Paul's innovations. On the other hand, a large part of Paul's
mission was to the Gentiles: he was trying to bring them in *tachat
kanfei ha-Shekhinah,* under the wings of *Shekhinah,* to convey
what he considered to be the real spiritual substance of Judaism
in the most accommodating way he could. So circumcision isn't
necessary if you want to convert, he declared, but you still must
perform the immersion in the *mikveh*—that is, baptism—that
we do in converting someone.

Over time our differences became tragic and deadly. Yet I believe that Judaism and Christianity were not so much mortal enemies but sparring partners, like Jacob and the angel that he
wrestled with, the angel that gave him the name Israel, "God
wrestler." Just as Jacob battled with the angel the night before
meeting Esau, emerging limping but victorious, knowing that he
could face his brother without fear, so did we emerge strength-
ened in some ways from the centuries of war with one of the
mightiest forces in civilization.

Despite all this warfare, Christian and other influences on Judaism are alive to this day. One cannot listen to synagogue music
without sensing the influence of sacred music from the church,
for instance. The seminaries that ordain our rabbis today teach
not only Torah but history and linguistics as well: this is a direct
influence from the churches and academies of Europe, imported

by the early Reform movement but now a part of seminary training in all Jewish denominations. In some ways the outside influences become more pervasive the higher we go. Our greatest early philosophers—Maimonides, Nachmanides, Gershonides, and others—were part of an intellectual ferment that included Muslim and Christian thinkers as well as the ancient Greeks.

So when a Christian proclaims what he or she knows to be good news (which is what *gospel* means), I want to hear it. In the Grace after Meals that traditional Jews say every day, we ask God to send us Elijah the prophet with the good news (*besorot tovot*) of redemption and consolation. Elijah, as we know from our legends, wears many garbs and disguises. Can we say that Yeshua of Nazareth, through whom countless people had a bridge to the living God, was not a guise of such good news?

We have some Jews today whose souls have been touched by the gospels, wonderful searching spirits who have felt the need to become hasidim of the Nazarene Rebbe and to follow the midrash of the Gospels. These Jews, too, are God-wrestling. I believe that we should regard them with an expanded sense of *ahavat Yisrael,* love of Israel, and that ostracizing them is wrong. But if you try to make Jesus a God, and say that everything in Torah and Yiddishkeit is already superceded, that for me is a different story. So I would draw a line there.

I cannot hear the good news of the Gospels if it addresses itself only to those who fully embrace Christianity. We each need to be able to share the good news that the other proclaims, without "power trips." Christians have always had their fundamentalists as we have ours, people who think that just because God gave them a snapshot of the universe in the year 33 C.E., they got the whole picture. They have a very good snapshot, but a snapshot tied in many ways to that particular time. Forcing today's reality into that same picture doesn't work. Original truths get distorted over time. Religions tend to emphasize one aspect over another. This is true on both sides of the fence. That is why we can learn from one another. Both Jews and Christians have aspects of our faiths that are well developed, and others that are either overdeveloped, top-heavy and rigid, or underdeveloped because we have seen only "through a glass darkly," in the words of Paul.

What we want here, to return to the metaphor of organs in the body, is sustainable permeability. If I, as the Jewish organ of the planet, am so fully closed off that I can't share with my environment, I will die. Similarly, if I am *too* permeable, I become invaded, overcome, homogenized into goop. Good membranes keep some stuff out and let other stuff through. Christian service to God is and must remain different from our own, yet we can find much harmony between the two.

How comfortable I feel celebrating with my Christian colleagues depends very much on their intention. Clearly, I would not participate if the priest sees in my participation a betrayal of Judaism. Our tradition considers this a *yehareg ve-al ya'avor,* a sin we should die for rather than commit. On the other hand, I was once invited to do a weekend for students in Vancouver with Paul van Buren, of blessed memory, the minister and theologian who was known for his work in advancing the understanding between our faiths. He participated with me on Shabbos, and I participated with him on Sunday. When it came his time to celebrate the mass, he used a challah and even made sure it was

kosher wine that he picked for the communion. When he got
to the verse from John 1:11, "He came unto his own [the Jews]
and they accepted him not," he said before the entire congregation, "This may be in the Gospels, but it is not the truth. Who
else accepted him at the time except the Jews? Who else were
his disciples?" With such a person I celebrate gladly.

Davening together is a very deep and wonderful way of sharing our love of God. I once spent Shabbos in Jerusalem with
Shlomo Carlebach. We wanted to go and daven at the Kotel, the
Western Wall, on Friday evening. Shlomo didn't like to daven
early, because early on Friday evening the Kotel is packed. He
figured if we waited until everyone was home eating gefilte fish,
the crowds would have thinned away. So Shlomo brought some
followers and we walked there together through the streets of
Jerusalem. At the Wall we found very few Jews, but rather a substantial group of Christians: priests, nuns, and laypeople. Shlomo
walked right over to them and invited them to join us.

The Christians are *"Peregrini italiani,"* they tell me—Italian
pilgrims. I greet them with *"Benedicite,"* and one of them says,
*"Dominus,"* and we get settled in. Shlomo sets up close to the
*mechitzah,* the separation between the men's and women's sections, as he always did, so the men and women could be as close
as we were allowed to be. He takes one table, I take another, and
behind us are the priests and nuns with their people. Then
Shlomo lifts up his voice and begins the Friday night prayer.
*"Lekhu neranena la-adonai*—Come, let us clamor joyfully to
God!" I call out to the priest behind me, "Psalm Ninety-five!"
and he says, *"Exultate Deo"* and gives the psalm number to his
followers. They open up their breviaries and we all daven along

together, the Jews in Hebrew and the pilgrims in Italian, all led by Shlomo's singing. Every time we came to a psalm I would call out the number and the pilgrims would follow. Instead of an "us" and a "them," we became a really strong "WE," all praying together like that. When we finally left, we said, "Gut Shabbos," and the priest said, *"Belle preghiere,"* beautiful prayers. The shared emotional space that we wove together around these psalms was really fantastic.

## Davening with Ishmael

The thing that allows people of different faiths to make a true and deep connection, whatever our differences, is our yearning and love for God. This is what we can keep coming back to. This is true for Muslims as well as Christians. The Shahadah, the quintessential Muslim declaration of faith, points to the same one God as we do. In Hebrew we express this Oneness as *achdut;* in Arabic they say *tawhid.* Both words stem from the same root: "One" is *echad* in Hebrew, *wahad* in Arabic.

With so many radicals on both sides talking war, I believe it is essential that we children of Abraham reach out more to one another. With Muslims, too, we can daven. I once searched out some Sufis, Islamic mystics, in Hebron, to try to celebrate together the Sufi ceremony known as *zhikr.* The sheikh asked me who I was. "I am a *mu'umin,* a believer in the One God," I said, and recited the Shahadah: "There is no God but God, and Muhammad is his prophet."

"How can you say that?" he asked.

I said, "Your ancestors, the sons of Ishmael, were in what you call *al-Jahiliyya,* the time of ignorance, until Muhammad, peace be upon him, came and brought you back to *tawhid,* faith in the oneness of God. So I believe Muhammad was a true messenger of God."

He said, "Let's not talk anymore. Bring in the music, let's do *zhikr* together." And they brought in drums and cymbals and we started doing the rhythmic chanting and movements that Sufis do to get close to God.

A Muslim gets just as excited as we do about Ibrahim, Abraham, being a friend of Allah. They also perform the awesome mitzvah of circumcision. When my boys were born and the time came for their bris, I invited a Muslim to hold the baby and to recite the Phatihah, the opening chapter of the Qur'an. I also had the privilege of being what we would call the *sandek* (godfather) at the bris of a Muslim baby boy in New Delhi. In the Jewish ceremony, when the baby is placed on the *sandek's* knees, we invoke the chair of Elijah the prophet. But that refers only to the Jewish covenant with God. In this case, though, I called upon our mutual father Abraham, and his sons—Isaac, father of the Jews, and Ishmael, father of the Arabs—as witnesses.

I hope that some day Jews and Muslims will meet in Hebron and celebrate the *yahrzeit* of our shared ancestors, Abraham and Sarah, and the others who are buried there and who are held dear by both. Hebron is the place of our shame at this point, home of extremists from both sides. Yet the word *Hebron* has the same root as the Hebrew *chaver,* friend. The Arabs call it *Al-Khalil,* which means the same thing. When we say kaddish together and pray

together for the memory of our shared parents, then we will finally remember that we, the descendants of Isaac and Ishmael,
are brothers. Utopian? Perhaps. But there are some Muslims,
particularly here in the United States, who are ready for this
kind of dialogue and in fact have already begun it. These are the
Muslims we need to be talking to.


## Bowing Down to Emptiness

We need to recognize, too, our debt to the religions of the Far
East. Shlomo Carlebach once gave a wonderful teaching about
this. I helped to organize an interfaith meeting in Berkeley some
years ago called "Torah and Dharma"—*dharma* being the Buddhist way and Torah being ours—and invited Reb Shlomo to
attend. He couldn't make it, but I asked him to give me a message to bring to the meeting.

Shlomo thought for a moment and then spoke. "We know that
we should seek knowledge from the lips of the priest (Malachi
2:7). We also know that it is forbidden for a priest to touch the
dead (Leviticus 21:1).

"The Ishbitzer Rebbe asks, Why is this so? Because if you
see the dead before you, if you touch the dead, you can't help
but be angry at God, the God who decreed that all who are
born must die. And when a teacher who is angry at God teaches
Torah, the Torah is bitter. In order to keep the teacher unpol-
luted, he must not touch the dead."

After the Holocaust, Shlomo said, all our teachers became
polluted. We are still polluted. How can we not be defiled by so
much death? So God, in His mercy, sent us teachers from the

Far East who were not polluted by death, and who did not feel the anger that we felt. And many of our young people, who thirsted for God but were somehow put off by our anger and defilement, turned to them for a word and a teaching on how to be close to God. So we owe these teachers our thanks.

This thirsting of our souls for God, for enlightenment, for self-realization, is not addressed by any aspect of halakhah, Jewish law. To describe this experience we would instead use the Hebrew word *t'shuvah*. Most often translated as repentance, t'shuvah also means the turning or re-turning of a soul to God. A soul thirsts for t'shuvah, the rabbis tell us, for two reasons. The first is fear, fear of punishment, the fear that the soul will suffer the results of its misdeeds. The second is love. It is true that Jews have flocked to the teachings of the East. One Zen teacher told me that more than half of his students were Jews. But the Jews who fill the ashrams and zendos clearly do not do so out of fear, but out of a deep longing and love for the universal, the absolute, the divine.

Of course, here, too, we can ask: Where does one draw the line? The statues of the Buddha, incense, mantras—isn't this idol worship? Isn't this *avodah zarah,* a form of worship that is alien to us?

Let us take Zen as an example. Surely we cannot say that the realization of the infinite, faceless Reality of all things—which is essentially what Zen is after—can be thought of as the worshipping of a heathen God. True, different branches of Zen include various sacramental acts. But as a Zen master once said, "Show me the Buddha and I will beat him with a stick." Given what I know of Zen's attitude to their rituals and forms, I can-

not object to them. To a certain extent we must let our souls be
our guides. The aspects of Zen that we generally feel more comfortable participating in tend to be those that are more universal.
Other aspects seem specifically Japanese and ethnic, even archaic
to our sensibilities. These are closer to the category of "alien
worship"—and tend to be the features that we feel less comfortable with anyway.

Here, too, it depends on the attitude of the non-Jewish people
we are sharing with. The Dalai Lama has told his non-Buddhist
followers that his aim is not to turn them into Tibetan Buddhists, but to encourage them to take the Buddhist teachings
home so that they can be better Jews, Christians, etc. The Hare
Krishnas, on the other hand, not only seem to fit every definition in Torah of idolatry; they also demand that their adherents
give up all other religions. This I would consider *avodah zarah,*
an alien form of worship.

I was teaching Jewish mysticism at Naropa, the university
founded by Tibetan Buddhist lama Chögyam Trungpa in Boulder, Colorado, when my father died. So I sat shiva in Boulder.
Allen Ginsberg, who was on the faculty there, participated in
the *minyan.* Just before the *Alenu* prayer, I asked him to read
Psalm 49, which is traditionally read at a shiva, and he read it
beautifully, as if he had written it himself. Then we said the *Alenu,*
including a sentence that appears in the traditional version I
grew up with: "for they bow down to Emptiness and the Void."
The rabbis meant this as a denigration of idol worship. But in
that moment, the davening, the shiva for my father, the Buddhist teachings of Chögyam Trungpa, the reading by Allen
Ginsberg—a Jew and devoted student of Tibetan Buddhism—

all these fused together in a single instant. I suddenly realized that "emptiness and void" was nothing but another perspective on what we call God, the Holy One, the King of King of Kings, whose highest attribute the Kabbalists call *ain,* No-thing—or as the Buddhists would say, no-thingness.

## THE CHALLENGE

There's an old Hasidic story about Reb Zushya, who told his students, as he lay dying, that he feared the heavenly court. His students were amazed. The saintly Reb Zushya! What did he possibly have to fear? Reb Zushya replied: "I am afraid God will say to me, 'Zushya! I did not expect that you would be Moses, or David, or Abraham. But don't you think you could have been more fully Zushya?'"

Looking back on his life as the boundaries of his own organism were dissolving, Zushya understood the challenge with clarity: to be most vigorously and alive-ly ourselves. His challenge is ours as well. As we wonder why and how to be Jewish, the challenge that faces us is to see ourselves not only as a Jew among Jews, as Zushya did, but from the perspective of a Jewish cell in the Jewish organ in the greater planetary organism of the world. In choosing to be Jewish—as often and as deeply as we can—we enrich not only ourselves but our organ in the planetary organism, our part in the great world drama, our instrument in the universal orchestra. This is also why we need a fuller, richer dialogue with those of other faiths: that they can be more fully Christians, Muslims, Hindus, Buddhists—and we can be more fully Jews.

CHAPTER 7

# THE JEWISH WORD FOR HOPE

1 WISH YOU'D EXPLAIN this business of the Messiah to me," a Jew asks his friend. "What exactly is supposed to happen?"

"Well, if Isaiah and Daniel are anything to go by, the wolf shall lie down with the lamb, the dead will be resurrected, the peoples from the four corners of the earth will be gathered to Jerusalem, and we'll all bring sacrifices as in biblical times," his friend replies.

"Resurrection of the dead!" The first Jew shudders. "What, like Ezekiel's valley of bones? Disgusting. You'll have to count me out on the sacrifices, too. It's a barbaric habit, and the sight of blood nauseates me. And I can't see this mass *aliyah* to Israel that you're talking about. The country is crowded enough already. Can you imagine the chaos at Ben Gurion Airport?" He goes on fretting like this for a while until his friend interrupts him.

"Listen," he says soothingly. "God saved us from Pharaoh. He saved us from Haman. Maybe he'll save us from Mashiach as well."

The idea of a Messiah makes us just as uneasy today, but for a different reason. While the guy in the joke was getting all upset by actually imagining the Mashiach's arrival, we have the opposite problem: we just can't picture it. The traditional Messianic vision, in which all the evildoers will get what's coming to them and will fry in the fire of Gehenna for ever and ever, and death will be swallowed up—this is not a vision of Messiah that we can take seriously. Few outside the very Orthodox communities believe that what Isaiah calls "the end of days" is going to come anytime soon, unless it is by nuclear Armageddon. I believe, though, that even today we Jews carry what I'd like to call a mashiach seed within us, an undying hope for the future that remains a crucial component of our spiritual lives.

Rabbi Rami Shapiro once described traditional Judaism as backing into the future with its eyes firmly fixed on the past. Broadly speaking, traditional Judaism sees us getting farther and farther away from our supreme moment of revelation: the giving of the Torah on Sinai. The more time passed from that point, this view holds, the less of that revelation we retained. So in the Babylonian Talmud we find, for example, the view that "If those who preceded us were angels, then we are mere humans; if they were humans then we are like donkeys" (Sabbath 112b). This was not just a matter of modesty, but of principle: a Talmudic sage, in elucidating and commenting on the Mishnah, the first collection of "Oral Torah," could not flatly contradict a Mishnaic sage. Even today, the impossibility of overturning halakhic decisions of the past stymies change in the Orthodox world—such as modernizing the ritual roles of women throughout Jewish life, to give but one crucial example.

Our Messianic hopes have always been infused with nostalgia for the "good old days." We end the Passover Seder with "Next year in Jerusalem!" envisioning an end-time with a re-created Temple just like the second one, complete with priests and sacrifices. On the Ninth of Av, the fast day that commemorates the destruction of the Temples—and, by tradition, the birthday of the Messiah—we close our reading of the book of Lamentations with the plea "*chadesh yamenu ke-kedem,* renew our days as of old." Our genius in revisioning the past has helped us preserve our values through centuries of persecutions and pressure. But that same genius also keeps us stuck in a cycle of seeking to re-create past glories.

Today we want a Judaism whose view of history includes not only the world that was, but the world that will be, a Judaism that will attract us joyfully into the future. Part 2 of this book has already examined two questions that I believe will be central to any Jewish future we can imagine. First, how can we elevate the care of our planet to the level of *avodat ha-Shem,* service to God? Second, how can we relate to other belief communities in a way that deepens our own faith as well as theirs, and that enriches human society and the planet as a whole? I would include both of these goals in any modern understanding of Mashiach, for Mashiach is simply the Jewish way of daring to hope that the future will be better than anything we have experienced so far.

Where does this hope come from? And where can it take us? How can the messianic seed in each of us help us imagine and bring about a better world? These are the questions we will be addressing here.

## PERFECT FAITH?

The constant yearning for a better world began long ago in response to our Diaspora experience. The first Jewish Diaspora resulted from the destruction of the First Temple by the Babylonians in 586 B.C.E. When the Babylonians were vanquished by the Medes and the Persians, the Persian king, Cyrus, decreed that the Jews could return to their homeland, eventually to build the Second Temple. Isaiah 45:1 describes Cyrus as the Lord's anointed—*meshicho,* God's Mashiach: "Thus saith the Lord to his anointed, to Cyrus, whose right hand I have held to subdue nations before him." Cyrus was, of course, not Jewish, but the sense was that God had specifically appointed the Persian ruler to save God's people. That glorious return was clearly imbued with early messianic feeling.

Our experience with flesh-and-blood messiahs since then has been more problematic. Jesus of Nazareth caused a bitter divide over the legacy of our faith that has not been healed to this day. Bar Kokhba, who sought to deliver the land of Israel from the oppressive hand of the Romans, was regarded even by his great contemporary Rabbi Akiva as the Messiah. But the disastrous uprising he led cost hundreds of thousands of Jewish lives and fatally weakened the entire Jewish presence in Judea. Messianic fervor in the wake of the Spanish expulsion centuries later centered on several figures, most notably Shabbetai Tzevi in the seventeenth century. When threatened with death for incitement, however, Shabbetai Tzevi and dozens of followers converted to Islam.

The failure of real-world messiahs no doubt convinced most of us that Messianic deliverance was best regarded as an article of faith, to be left in the hands of God. When Maimonides (1135–1204) articulated his Thirteen Principles of Faith, faith in the coming of the Messiah was among them. In the formulation still recited by many Jews today, each Principle starts out "*Ani ma'amin,* I believe with perfect faith."

*I believe with perfect faith*
*In the coming of the Messiah.*

Alone among the other Thirteen Principles, however, this one betrays a hint of desperation.

*Though he tarries, in spite of all*
*I will wait for him every day and expect his coming.*

"Though he tarries, in spite of all." Oy, how our ancestors were hounded for their beliefs. How few rays of hope they had. Throughout those dark ages, only faith—unreasoning faith, faith that flew in the face of centuries of persecution, faith in a miraculous deliverance—gave them the strength to live. Jews who were marched to the gas chambers for the crime of having Jewish blood in their veins spent their last breaths singing that *Ani ma'amin:* "In spite of all, I will wait for him." And still he tarried.

The seed of messianic hope that lives on in us today expresses itself differently. We live in a world with a Jewish state and a Jewish army, developments our ancestors could not have imagined. Yes, anti-Semitism still exists, but our freedom of religion is protected in every civilized country. Today's messianic hope rests not on a passive hope for a better world, but on the active urge to *create* that world. Even the Jewish Communists of the 1930s spoke of replacing the traditional Messiah with a *royte mashiach,* a Red Messiah. Broadly speaking, the more free of oppression Jews became in modern times, the more that urge has asserted itself. Today, thank God, we have every reason to hope that a vision of a better world *can* be translated into reality, and that this transformation can begin now. In this view we are all Messianists. We all carry the sparks of Mashiach. We all, in our own unassuming ways, can work to improve the world.

Now, it is easy to imagine a utopia that will have nothing to do with being Jewish. Ultimately, yes, we want to bring about a healing that is bigger than the Jewish idea of Mashiach. A generic utopian vision may be the ultimate ideal, but it loses the *saltz,* the *schmaltz,* the ethnic flavor. That's not what we waited twenty-five hundred years for. In any future I can imagine, I believe we Jews will still have a contribution to make as Jews. So the vision of the future that I want to offer to the world is a Jewish vision. How can a specifically Jewish way of imagining the future help us bridge the gap between the world we live in and the world we would like to see? To help answer this question, let us examine a few teachings that will give us a better sense of what Jews have meant by "Mashiach" through the centuries.

# DREAM SPACE

Perhaps the most famous descriptions of the end-time are from
the prophet Isaiah. "The wolf shall dwell with the lamb, and the
leopard shall lie down with the kid, and the calf and the young
lion and the fatling together, and a little child shall lead them"
(Isaiah 11:6). These images portray a peaceable kingdom, a world
that has left all aggression behind. The rabbis echoed Isaiah's
idyllic imaginings. "In the future to come," they said, "all people
will understand the language of birds and trees." Clearly, such a
vision could not be fulfilled in a world with the same biological
rules as our own. We sense again here a nostalgia for our most
distant past, the Garden of Eden, a nostalgia Isaiah projects into
the future, picturing a perfect union with nature that only our
first ancestors, Adam and Eve, ever knew.

Isaiah's vision of predators and prey lying down together was
clearly meant to extend to Israel and the nations as well. "[A]nd
they shall beat their swords into plowshares, and their spears into
pruninghooks: nation shall not lift up sword against nation, neither shall they learn war any more" (Isaiah 2:4). One day, Isaiah
assures his listeners, the nations will recognize Israel's vision of
the One God who rules over nature and the world as well. Most
synagogue goers will recognize the sentence we sing in taking
the Torah out of the Ark: "*Ki mi-tzion teitzei torah u-d'var Adonai
mi-Yerushalayim,* for Torah will be broadcast from Zion and the
word of God from Jerusalem" (Isaiah 2:3). Yet these words shall
be uttered not by Israel, according to Isaiah, but by the nations

that go up to the "mountain of the Lord" in Jerusalem "at the end of days." Other verses reiterate this theme:

"My house will be called the house of prayer for *all* people" (Isaiah 56:7).

"Even from them [the gentiles] will I take Levites and priests" (Isaiah 66:21).

Isaiah and his contemporaries must have lived at an extraordinary time. For reasons that are still not clear to us, they were part of a great explosion of consciousness that scholars have called the Axial Age, an era that included Socrates, Plato, Aristotle, Zarathustra, Mahavira, Gautama Buddha, Lao-tzu, and Confucius. Though Isaiah's vision was not without a hint of triumphalism, he shared the intuition with the most exalted thinkers in civilizations around the globe that at the very highest level, ultimate truth lies in the *yichud* place, the place of union.

When Isaiah tells us that "the earth shall be filled with knowledge of God as water covers the sea" (Isaiah 11:9), what can this mean? The water and the sea are identical. It's like the English expression that we can't see the forest for the trees. One answer: When the Messiah comes, the world will be filled with such an awareness of God that we will finally realize that God and the world are one and the same. We will recognize that everything is God. The apocalyptic prophet Daniel echoes this sense of universal knowledge. "Understanding shall be increased," he says. Many things "shall become clear and white . . . the wise shall understand" (Daniel 12:4, 10). Things now opaque will become transparent. Things that now obscure our understanding will be cleared up. We will become enlightened.

But such passages broadcast another very important message

that we have not touched on yet: the vital importance of dreaming. Our visions for a better world can never really get off the ground if we remain imprisoned in our calm, rational, cortex space. What our prophets and rabbis did in entering the messianic space, and what we need to do in imagining a better future, is to dream. The soul can visualize perfections that have not yet been manifested in this world. Eternity is such a wonderful mind-stretcher.

## DOORWAY:
## DREAMING OF A BETTER WORLD

Let us enter a messianic dream space together.

If I could but live to see the end-time, the rabbis tell me, I would understand the speech of animals and birds. I stare out the window and begin to space out. I imagine myself in the middle of the woods, and it is time for the afternoon prayers. I want to pray in a minyan, but nobody else is there. I see squirrels, though, and birds, and butterflies. They serve as my minyan. I imagine a halakhah of the future that will explain how to daven with dolphins. I imagine all the pack animals of the world standing unburdened at a future Temple, neighing and braying in unison. How I long to be in that number, when those saints come marching in!

Think of an area in your life that you wish was going better: your work, your relationship with your partner, your kids, your friends, your body—something about which you tend to say, "Why can't this be such and such a way?" This time, though, try to flip around your usual way of thinking. Instead of "Why can't this be the way I envision it?" think, "I can imagine a different life, one in which . . ." What does that life look like?

Know that the divine spark in each of us is not bound by the restrictions of time and space. Time is not only linear. On higher levels, in dimensions many times to the power of ours, time folds in on itself and makes many more connections than are apparent to us.

Rabbi Isaac Luria, the holy Ari of Safed, taught that a Jewish soul must return to this life until it walks perfectly in the ways of God. This teaching tells me that someday the soul of Zalman will complete all its incarnations and become the fully and completely realized Zalman. This is what people call the higher mind, the mind that knows. No guru, no rebbe, can take me into full realization the same way as the realized Zalman can. Maybe, by going deep inside of myself, I can have a *yechidus,* a moment of complete union, with that fully realized Zalman.

For my soul, unbound by the strictures of linear time, knows that that Zalman exists somewhere even today. Waiting for me. Rooting for me at times. Sending me care packages. In the mystical realms, where time folds in on itself, an incarnation in the twenty-fourth century can touch my soul where it is today and transmit needed wisdom. In those mystical realms, too, I can send myself care packages to the past. Every so often, in an especially *she-hechiyanu* moment—thank you so much, God, for sustaining me to see this day!—I have remembered a day when I was so despairing, so lost, and sent a care package back to the self I was then, saying, "Take a glimpse of where I am right now, in your future. Don't give up hope." I have visited myself at my bris. "Nu, Zalmaleh, someday you're gonna be a rebbe. Relax, it's all right, you will get over it." And I believe that a future, even more fully realized Zalman is sending me care packages, too.

Can you leave the strictures of time behind and connect with your fully realized self? What messages is that self sending you?

Can we expand such meditations outward? Can we imagine a fully realized planet, a world completely merged with the divine? In asking such a question we are not looking for a specific endpoint, but for a direction. Without a higher vision pulling us into the future we are like the two characters in Thomas Pynchon's novel *V*: "Where are we going?" one asks.

"The way we're headed," the other replies.

Our searching souls are not satisfied with such randomness, such pointlessness. They demand more meaning, more purpose. The soul wants to orient itself toward ever higher ascents. In English we might ask, "Which way is true north?" As Jews we would ask, "Which way is *mizrach,* the East?" Point me, the soul says, toward the holy city. Point the way out of the night and toward the dawn. Let me look toward that place and listen, that I may hear the call more clearly.

## LIVING IN THE FUTURISTIC NOW

Rabbi Israel Meir Ha-Cohen, the Chofetz Chayim, taught that a Jew should demand the coming of Mashiach with the confidence of a laborer demanding his daily wages. Beyond this insistence that things must and will get better, however, we find nothing but inconsistencies and contradictions. But this is not only because all futuristic visions are bound to be just speculation. What seems to us to be inconsistency and contradiction are part and parcel of the Jewish concept of Mashiach. Mashiach does not ask us to find a way around contradictions. It asks us to rest in them.

When two opposing sides had argued themselves to a draw, the Talmud would end that line of discussion with the acronym TeYKU, which meant "the Tishbite will resolve all questions and problems." The Tishbite was a traditional name for Elijah the Prophet. In essence, then, this means: "You wait, when the prophet Elijah returns, all the contradictions and problems will be resolved and become clear." TeYKU asks us to allow the tension of a contradiction without seeking to reduce it. The idea of TeYKU puts us in a situation like a Zen student presented with a koan, a seemingly illogical or self-contradictory situation like "What is the sound of one hand clapping?" Koans reconstellate the mind into a new understanding, a new harmony of opposites. From the creative tension of such contradictions, new insights arise. Elijah is supposed to come three days before Mashaich, but we do not need to wait until the end of days. Israelis use the expression *gilui Eliyahu,* an "Elijah revelation," to mean a flash of insight, an epiphany. The lesson for us here is that allowing such creative contradictions may reward us with new and higher insights.

In Hebrew the name of Adam, the first human, is spelled *aleph, dalet, mem.* Some say the letters stand for Adam, David,

Mashiach—the direct line of redemption. According to legend, the soul of Adam contained the souls of all humans ever after. When that first soul reached for the fruit of the Tree of Knowledge, all the souls in the world reached with it. Only one flew away like a bird from where the others clustered. This soul did not taste from the Tree of Knowledge: it did not become a part of the good/evil, either/or universe. This soul is the soul of Mashiach.

Our either/or minds might say, "Wait a minute. Wishing for a better world is all very well. But what about the lessons we are learning from Buddhism and meditation about staying with the present moment, accepting it, seeing what emerges from it? All this yearning and dreaming from our persecuted past takes us away from that. At the same time, of course, I do have hopes for a better world. I even hope that I myself might improve the world in some small way. Which implies that I am not satisfied with the world as it is! How do I reconcile those two philosophies?"

Our Mashiach seed tells us, "That seeming contradiction is a fruitful one. Rest in it as long as you can. Of course we should be rooted in the present: Jewish practice is, in many ways, all about being anchored in the here and now as deeply and appreciatively as we can. *And,* at the very same time, never lose your active hope to bring about a better world."

The contradictions that Mashiach embodies emerge from a story that the Baal Shem Tov used to tell. Once there was a merchant of diamonds, and he had a very precious stone. This stone was the special obsession of a jewel thief, who tried every way he could think of to get the diamond from the merchant, without success. For years he dogged the merchant's footsteps. Finally their travels threw them together in the same inn, far from any other town. By chance the innkeeper had only one room available, and the room had only one bed.

So the two men bring their bags up to the room and get settled in. First one gets washed up, then the other gets washed up, and they go down to eat. At the table the *gonif* slips a Mickey Finn into the merchant's drink, and the poor guy barely makes it up the stairs. He falls onto the bed in such a cataleptic stupor that the *gonif* can not only ransack his belongings but can touch every part of his body without fear. The *gonif* goes through everything, looks in every nook and cranny. He searches for hours into the night—but he just can't find the diamond. Finally in utter frustration he sinks down next to the merchant and goes to sleep.

In the morning the merchant stretches and climbs unsteadily out of bed. The thief is still completely asleep, mouth open, snoring. So the merchant goes over to the thief's bag, where the night before he had hidden the diamond, and fishes it out of a side pocket. It was the only place he thought the thief wouldn't look.

The Baal Shem Tov used to say that the Master of the Universe hid the spark of Messiah *bai dem gonif in peckel,* in the bag of the thief. The forces of evil in the universe, the Baal Shem taught, don't want the Mashiach to come, and put every kind of obstacle in the way. So the Master of the Universe hides him where evil wouldn't think to look. Evil is still very much alive in the world today, whether in the torture chambers of despotic regimes, the rapacious behavior of our own corporations, domestic violence, or the neglect of millions of starving children. Our hopes can be so easily crushed. Yet in this very world is hope hidden, the Baal Shem Tov's simile insists, and in this very world we can find and nurture it.

How, according to tradition, did God hide the Mashiach? Isn't he supposed to descend directly from King David himself? Yes. But take a look at King David's pedigree. From a traditional Jewish point of view, David has several strikes against him before he is even born. He is the tenth-generation descendant of an illicit union between Judah, son of Jacob the patriarch, and Judah's daughter-in-law Tamar—whom Judah slept with because he thought she was a harlot (Genesis 38). David's great-grandmother was not born Jewish: she was Ruth of Moab, the hostile nation whose king hired Balaam to curse the tribes of Israel (Numbers 22). Another midrash explains David's declaration that "In sin my mother conceived me" (Psalms 51:7) as referring to a tryst that David's father, Jesse, had with a concubine.

The Messianic line hardly improved after David's generation. David's son Solomon was the daughter of Bathsheba, a woman David obtained through adultery and murder, crimes for which, as the prophet Nathan told him, "the sword will not depart from your house." Solomon built the Temple and brought forty years of peace to Israel, but his descendants displayed every kind of venality and impiety.

From the standpoint of pedigree, then, the Mashiach is very far from glatt kosher. The Messianic soul, on the other hand, is the ultimate in kosherness: it will make the whole world kosher! How can this tension be resolved? How could such a flawed body ever sustain such holiness? This tension was not lost upon the Jews—or the Christians, for that matter. The Christian solution was to clean up their Mashiach's pedigree. Jesus was descended

from the house of David but he was "conceived by the Holy
Ghost," as the Apostles' Creed says, "born of the Virgin Mary"—
who herself was immaculately conceived, her soul infusing her
body "exempt from all stain of original sin," as Pope Pius IX declared. The Jewish solution, on the other hand, was to let the
tension stand.

I once heard Reb Menachem Mendel of Lubavitch expound-
ing on a commentary on the verse, "And God's spirit hovered
on the face of the waters" (Genesis 1:2). This is the second verse
of the creation story, describing the scene before creation began. The words *God's spirit,* the commentary says, are the name
of the Mashiach. How do we understand this? the Rebbe asked.
Could this mean that the Messiah's name preceded creation itself? He explained: A name connects the body to the soul. The
soul of Mashiach is so high that it didn't participate in the sin of
the Tree of Knowledge. The body of Mashiach is so low that it's
barely kosher. Fusing such a body to such a soul required a name
so primal that it had to precede the creation of the world. Nothing in the created world as Judaism normally understands it could
have resolved such a contradiction.

"And God's spirit"—the name and essence of Mashiach—
"hovered on the face of the waters." Have you ever seen a hen
sitting on her eggs? Of course we can put the eggs in a machine,
an incubator, but that's not what's happening with the mama hen.
She sits on those eggs and says, "Life . . . Life . . . Go into those
chicks. . . ." For days she sits there, sending that message down.
That's the sense I get from the hovering of God's spirit in Genesis. The Hebrew word for "hovers," *merachefet,* is feminine. We
feel the *Shekhinah,* the feminine face of God, brooding . . .

brooooooding over the waters to coax up life. One cell. More cells. We feel a constant sending down of revelation like a broody hen pushing down life, coaxing us into greater awareness, greater connectedness.

I believe the *Shekhinah* has been sending down that revelation from the first moment of creation. This is not the single overwhelming revelation of Torah from Sinai, whose echoes have ever since deteriorated with time. This is Torah that's coming to us right now. The seeds of this revelation are inside and all around us. Yes, our present world is flawed, but redemptive gems are hidden in its every corner, just as in the Baal Shem Tov's story, eluding all attempts to steal them away. We see a hint of this very different view of history and human potential contained in this quote from Talmud: "Six thousand years the world will exist; two thousand chaos, two thousand Torah, two thousand the days of the Messiah" (Avodah Zarah 9a). This timeline imagines us ascending through the ages to ever higher levels of understanding. What we see here is not entropy but an *evolution* of consciousness, a continuous loosening up and releasing of revelation, a revelation we are accumulating day by day. Sinai pulls us back to the past, but Mashiach pulls us into the future. The mashiach seed in each of us dreams of a better future even while remaining rooted in the imperfect present.

Mystics of other faiths have shared this view. Teilhard de Chardin (1881–1955), for example, was a French Jesuit paleontologist. Both a scientist and a priest, Teilhard de Chardin believed that the scientific and spiritual views of the world came together in Darwin's theory of evolution. He saw direction and purpose in the emergence of life from inorganic matter and of consciousness from life. Our world, he believed, is evolving toward a yet higher form of conciousness, a universal consciousness of the divine, a "divinization" of the planet.

Every age seeks to translate the mashiach message anew. The traditional Jewish trappings of the Messianic idea—whether he's pictured as "poor and riding on an ass" (Zechariah 9:9) or arriving "with the clouds of heaven" (Daniel 7:13)—are just that: trappings. They are the symbolic costume that our search for ever-increasing enlightenment wears in every production of the Messiah play. They clothe in a mythic robe that wonderful urge, that thrust that pulls, pushes, takes us into the future, deploying us to see the world with consciousness, taking us to higher and higher levels of understanding and caring and connection. In ancient times our hope for a better world wore the robes of King Messiah. In recent times it waved a red flag and sang the "Internationale." Today it speaks the language of inclusiveness, or *tikkun olam*. Every age tries to figure out how to translate that hope for the future into process, into action.

How can we help to bring about that transformation even while going on with our lives? In the Talmud there's a category of Jewish law known as *hilkheta le-mashichah,* halakhic rulings that demand too much of us in our current spiritual state but will take effect when the Mashiach comes. Rabbi Arthur Waskow asks: Why should we wait that long? Let us begin to live up to our highest aspirations. Let's "pre-tend," in the sense of *tending* toward a goal before we achieve that, before we *are* that.

Judaism already has a sense of this. We call Shabbos *me-ein olam ha-ba,* a taste of the world to come, and try to live that day as if Mashiach had already come. Reb Shmuel of Lubavitch wrote that every person should spend and experience at least fifteen minutes a day living like a *tzaddik gamur,* a complete tzaddik, a perfectly righteous person. In these brief periods spent in the presence of God, we can begin to capture a sense of not having to strive, of being there already.

## DOORWAY: FIFTEEN MINUTES IN THE PRESENCE OF GOD

We start with a phrase: *Shiviti ha-Shem le-negdi tamid,* I hold God before me always. Spend a few minutes just breathing in the presence of that thought.

For the next fifteen minutes I want to live in the service of God. My ego is totally aligned with the service of God: I don't want to do anything else. I have no other strivings at this point.

Slowly I embrace an attitude of gratitude. I think of a verse like Psalm 116:12, which we recite in the *Hallel* prayer on festivals: "What can I give back to God? His every blessing is upon me."

I say, "*Ribbono shel olam,* Master of the Universe, I love you. Thank you for this life. I love you." I open my heart to the mitzvah of *ahavat ha-Shem,* loving God.

I go deeper. I know no separation exists between me and God and the universe, and so I say, as the Kabbalists did, "*Echad, yachid, u-m'yuchad,* all is One." I open my mind to the mitzvah of *yichud ha-Shem,* of unification, of fusing all reality into One.

. . .

I turn my thoughts to those around me, knowing that they are the same stuff and substance as myself. I remember what I can do to hurt people. I know I may have done some of these things. I spend some time in t'shuvah, in helping myself and the universe repent and be restored from that hurt.

I remember the mitzvah of reaching out to our fellow humans with love. "*Ve-ahavta le-rei'akha kamokha,* love your friend as dearly as yourself" (Leviticus 19:18). How can I hope to ever truly fulfill this mitzvah? Sitting here in silence, I send out my love to everyone around me, those I know and those I don't know.

Or I might remember somebody whom I need to call and make a connection with, and spend fifteen minutes doing that.

I make an agreement with myself: whatever I can do today to improve the world, let me not turn away from doing it.

## FAIRNESS AND *GEMILUT CHASADIM*

In trying to bring a better tomorrow, we want to take our spirituality beyond our private thoughts and out into the real world. We have stressed the importance of improving our relationship to the planet and enriching our relationship with other faiths, but here I want to talk about *menschlichkeit.* In day-to-day Jewish life, one of the highest ways to praise somebody was to say, "He's a real *mensch.*" A real *mensch* was more than just an upstanding member of his community. It meant a person who acted decently and fairly to his fellows, and brought an extra helping of *gemilut chasadim,* or human kindness, as well. When Mr. Aaron Feuerstein kept three thousand workers on the payroll after a fire at Malden Mills put them out of work, we witnessed an act of a true *mensch.*

Imagine a world that is infused with a great deal more *menschlichkeit,* more fairness and *gemilut chasadim,* than our world embodies today. So many exchanges in the world involve some form of inequality, some form of friction between haves and have-nots, or have-mores and have-lesses. We find such inequalities everywhere we look: in the workplace, in marriages, even between sovereign nations. A has more money, more power, more knowledge, more authority, more confidence, more clout, than B. So A calls the shots, and B complies. In the process B loses something of him- or herself and is demeaned. I believe that reducing the friction between ourselves and others is real Mashiach work. The word *Mashiach,* after all, means "anointed one," one who has been anointed with oil as the sign of his kingship. (The first kings of Israel, Saul and David, were anointed by the prophet Samuel, while Solomon was anointed by David's priest Zadok.) What does oil do? It reduces friction. We get a sense here of Mashiach as something that greases the wheels of the universe. Newborn babies are Messiah-ed in this way, coming into the world anointed with white vernix, that wonderful sliding, gliding material. In this sense everyone who's born is already a mashiach, an anointed one!

Now, mediating the friction between unequals is something that Torah pays a great deal of attention to, especially in the economic sphere. The laws of Torah strive to create an environment that does not allow someone to take something for himself alone. For example: Torah required a person who owned a field to leave the harvest in one corner of the field for the poor to gather. Furthermore, in harvesting the field, a certain number of sheaves were bound to escape the harvester's hand. These, too, Torah says, were to be left for the poor. The owner was not to gather in those crops for the poor: the landless had the dignity and the right to come and cut the corn for themselves. Other tithes and contributions added to this social safety net. A "temp," or day laborer, had to be paid by sundown, every day. A garment received as security for a loan must be returned for the night if its owner needed it to keep warm.

These laws were never restricted to persons already reduced to a state of total dependency. They sought to guarantee certain dignities for all those at the lower ends of the economic ladder and to maintain that dignity by enabling them to do as much as possible for themselves.

Torah does not begrudge a person success: the patriarchs Abraham, Isaac, and Jacob, for instance, our quintessential model *mensches,* all rose with God's help to positions of wealth and dignity as herdsmen. What Torah emphasizes is that the benefits that we reap from the common soil of the community, as it were—what we might call today the marketplace—provide an opportunity for us to serve the community in return.

What would we call such legislation today? A tax. Some politicians in our country would have us believe that every dollar paid in taxes is an imposition. Torah says to the contrary: paying taxes is a mitzvah! Living in a country like ours without paying taxes would be like enjoying a year-round membership in a country club without paying dues. Yes, we would like more control over how our tax money is used. If we were able to devote our tax contribution to feeding the hungry rather than waging war, then we might feel the mitzvah of a clean tax return. But let's be clear: that portion of our taxes that supports the general welfare of society, particularly society's have-nots, is a mitzvah from Torah's point of view.

Building and maintaining a fair society is as fundamental to Torah as anything else in the Jewish gestalt. We seek a sense of "justice, justice shalt thou pursue" (Deuteronomy 16:20)— justice for both sides of every transaction, justice both in earthly eyes and in the eyes of heaven. When biblical society forgot these laws of human fairness in their zeal to do right by God, the prophets brought them up short. Why should God give a damn about your sacrifices, Isaiah says bluntly, if you neglect the widow and the orphan?

The laws we have been discussing here were all *mitzvot ha-t'luyot ba-aretz,* mitzvot required only of Jews living in the Holy Land under Jewish rule. But Jewish law extended the sense of fairness that these laws embodied to Diaspora life as well. When Maimonides codified the whole body of Jewish law in the twelfth century, for example, the old law regarding the corner of the field yielded a number of principles regarding how society's "have-mores" should extend a helping hand to "have-lesses":

- How society can set a floor beneath which a person should not be forced to sink on account of money

- How not to give in such a way that the person receiving is reduced to feeling like a *shmattah,* a rag
- How to give what the person needs, while requiring them to help themselves to the extent that they are able

Maimondes extended these principles to define an entire hierarchy of *tzedekah* (giving). At the top of this hierarchy were loans that enabled the recipient to become self-sufficient. Next were various types of anonymous gifts, to preserve the dignity of the recipient. Face-to-face transactions, such as dropping money into a beggar's cup, were near the bottom.

Jews took these precepts seriously. For example, when I was not quite into my teens, there was a man who came on Friday mornings to hire me. My job was to help him do the mitzvah *matan be-seter,* to make a gift in hiding. Knowing that certain families did not have enough for Shabbos, he would send me to deposit a bag on their doorstep. I would sneak up to the door, drop the bag, knock on the door, and run. Then I would hide at the end of the hallway and watch to make sure the package really reached its intended destination and did not get taken by the wrong party. This man was so concerned that no one should know who he was, as Maimonides recommended, that he paid me hush money for delivering those parcels!

The man modeled in his behavior an important principle of *menschlichkeit.* The kind of world that we want to see, and the kind of world Torah tries to create, is based on more than just fairness. We need an additional layer of mercy, charity, and love in all our human dealings. We need compassion. Not compassion as in pity, but *com-passion,* the realization that every person we see is created in the same divine image as we are. Rabbi Israel Salanter, leader of the so-called *musar,* or ethics, movement, was once visiting a well-to-do householder. When the time came to wash his hands before making a blessing over the bread, the wealthy man was surprised to notice that Reb Salanter used only a bare minimum of water to fulfill the mitzvah. "Please, Rabbi," he said, "use as much water as you want!"

"How does the water get here?" the Rabbi asked him. "Your maid carries it. I don't want to be *frum* (pious) on her shoulders."

Most world religions hold up a model for compassion. The sacred heart of Jesus is the Christian face of cosmic compassion. Muslim's favorite name for Allah is the Merciful, the Compassionate. When Hasidim talk about a *tzaddik,* a quintessentially righteous person, we're talking about the same thing, about compassion at work. Hindus and Buddhists talk about *karuna,* compassion or loving-kindness. The Buddhist figure of the bodhisattva, a being who says, "I will not go into my liberation until the very last sentient being on earth has made it," is the Buddhist address for cosmic compassion. What we are all aiming for is the realization that all individual souls are but expressions of a single Soul. Doing the inner work necessary to realize that, and translating that realization to action, is what redemption is all about.

How do we put that realization to work? The Jewish answer is: through *gemilut chasadim.* The simplest and most popular translation of *gemilut chasadim* is deeds of loving-kindness. When we recognize an act of *gemilut chasadim* we say, "Oy! Such a mitzvah." *Gemilut chasadim* flows from the divine attribute known as *chesed,* the welcoming, accepting love manifested in Abraham and Sarah. *Chesed* approximates the love that in Greek is called *agape,* divine love. Paul of Tarsus describes this kind of love in his epistle to the Corinthians:

> Love is long suffering and kind. It does not envy, nor make much of itself. It does not behave rudely, not seeks its own; is not easily provoked; thinks no evil. Does not rejoice in iniquity, but rejoices in the truth. Bears all things, believes all things, hopes all things, endures all things. (1 Corinthians 13:4–7)

*Chesed* is like a good-morning smile that lights up an elevator full of workers on the way to the office. It can infuse our relations not only with family and friends, but with complete strangers as well. *Agape* and *chesed* are sometimes translated as charity, but that doesn't really capture it. Charity we give only to those in need. *Chesed* goes everywhere. It permeates all our dealings. Thoreau captures something of this quality in *Walden:*

> I would not subtract anything from the praise that is due to philanthropy, but merely demand justice for all who by their lives and works are a blessing to mankind. I do not value chiefly a man's uprightness and benevolence, which are, as it were, his stem and leaves. . . . I want the flower and fruit of a man; that some fragrance be wafted over from him to me, and some ripeness flavor our intercourse. His goodness must not be a partial and transitory act, but a constant superfluity, which costs him nothing and of which he is unconscious. (*Walden,* "Economy")

Charity gives money to a beggar but he still remains a beggar. *Chesed* is different. Turgenev tells a great story about how he walks across a bridge and meets a beggar begging. He reaches into his pocket for a coin but finds he does not have a cent to give. So he turns to the man and says, "I am so sorry, brother, I do not have anything to give to you."

"You have just given me something," the man replies. "You called me brother."

We get the sense that *chesed* rests first and foremost on truly seeing another, rather than dismissing him with a label, whether that label be "Oh, a beggar" or "Oh, there's John." One of the least expensive but most energy-producing forms of *gemilut chasadim* is to walk over to another person and say, "*Shalom aleikhem*, peace be with you, friend," in a way that really sees that person and lets her know that she is being seen and embraced.

*Gemilut* is the word that turns individual acts of *chesed* into an entire network. It derives from the same Hebrew word as the phrase *yachas gomlin*, meaning a relationship of mutuality and reciprocity. *Gemilut* is the activity that creates the I-Thou relationship that Martin Buber describes. You sustain me and I sustain you. Or: you act toward me with *chesed*, I do the same to the next person I meet, and it will come around to you again. In this way *gemilut chasadim* is woven throughout the fabric of society. Such a vision helps us understand why the rabbis saw *gemilut chasadim* as one of the three pillars of existence: "Three things sustain the world: Torah, the service of God, and *gemilut chasadim*" (Pirke Avot 1:3).

We usually say a blessing before doing a mitzvah. When it

comes to charity, to helping another person, we don't say a blessing. Why? First, the rabbis recognized that in saying a blessing we would in some way be separating ourselves from the person we're trying to help, turning to God up there rather than the person down here. Instead, we should visualize God in the person who needs help. Second, when people are hungry you can't futz around: "Nu, listen, I'll soon give you something to eat, but in the meantime I have to go to the *mikveh* so I can say the blessing." *Gemilut chasadim* doesn't need *mikveh,* and it doesn't need to make a *b'rakhah.* When people need help, they need it now.

## DOORWAY:
### THE *CHESED* OF HONEST FEEDBACK

Truly reaching out to another person is not easy. To help and reach out to someone, as everyone knows, we need to have empathy. But empathy works on so many levels: the sensory level, the feeling level, the thinking level, the intuitive level. It's like a parent reaching out to her child. She opens not only her arms, but her heart, mind, and soul as well. If you can vibrate with a person on these levels, you can really help them, because they will *know* that you are there for them. A sort of *boinnnngggg!* happens, a shared resonance, a believability. So many times, when we're in a troubled place, we get to feeling like the words in the old spiritual, "Nobody knows the troubles I've seen." Nobody comes to meet me in that lonely place where I am. We want someone to say, "I know where you're coming from"—and we want to *believe* it.

Again, this goes far beyond acts of material charity. Almost everyone remembers times that they have felt out of step with everyone around them. Every time we rub up against the world we seem to cause friction. Now, imagine reaching out for a drop of that miraculous friction-reducing mashiach oil, a drop of *gemilut chasadim*. Imagine you could say to a friend, "Do me a favor. I'm confused. I don't quite know what I stand for these days. I'm never sure how I come across to people, whether the message that I think I'm projecting is in fact what people really see. I want to make a change. I want to steer better. Can you tell me what kind of person you see when you look at me? Can you mirror myself back to me, give me your gentle but honest assessment of how I'm doing?"

What we are looking for is not hard to explain: it is simply honest and compassionate feedback: "This is what I see. This is how you are coming across in my view. If you can use my eyes to help you be the person you want to be, then I lend them to you." I do this with two or three friends before every Rosh ha-Shanah. If we can, we meet in person; otherwise we talk on the phone. At one point in our lives, for example, workaholism was the issue. Then the feedback was something like, "Listen, if you keep going like this it's going to kill you. Even if you never do anything else in your life, you've already done a lot. Stop pushing so hard." Another time I was complaining to a Sufi friend; things at home were not as good as I wanted them to be. He said, "Tell me, do you pray for your wife?" That simple feedback gave me a real *zetz*.

Lending our eyes so a friend can better accomplish her own desires is just as precious a mitzvah as lending money or things. How else can we really know where we are in life? How else can we find out what we truly stand for, whether the message we think we are sending out into the world is indeed what others are receiving? Giving things is important. But giving intangibles—time, energy, attention, insight—is also a great *gemilut chesed*. And it needs to be done with the same consideration for the dignity of the recipient. We are not doling out insight to the needy, but helping a friend stand squarely on her own two feet in the world.

What would the world look like if all human relations were characterized by simple *gemilut chasadim?* Imagine a world in which everybody does mitzvahs. Everyone who needs a mitzvah finds the one they need; everyone who wants to do a mitzvah finds someone who needs one. As our soul's memory of higher worlds is what sustains us in faith, the vision of a world transformed by *gemilut chasadim* can sustain us in hope, the kind of hope our ancestors described with the word *mashiach*.

True, we see things every day that make us sad and angry: every day the world falls short of what it could be. But we should not forget to look at the world we live in, too, with *chesed*. The world is in daily need of our *farginnen,* our well-wishing, our openhearted blessing. We need to hold our world, with all its grave disappointments and pain and destruction, close to our heart and say, "I *fargin* you, world. I bless you. I wish you the best. I accept you just as you are. I don't want to be angry with you. I want to love you for what you are and might still become."

# A FINAL BLESSING

ONE OF THE greatest needs this planet has for healing is blessing. It is underblessed. Underblessed reality is like empty calories.

A blessing enhances the possibilities for good. Like an enzyme for growth, like a catalyst in a chemical process, blessings serve to help a living process surmount the barriers that obstruct it.

We need people who have learned to offer blessings. Elders are often the best people to do this. I want to ask the reader who followed me to this point to join with me in blessing the planet, the next generation, all species, all good intentions in people's hearts, all those who face burnout in their service to others, to the scientists and physicians who work on finding cures for cancer and AIDS, for prisoners in our penal systems who want to start a new and better life, for the prisoners of conscience to be freed, for warring nations to find the way to peace and cooperation, for those whose time has come to leave their body to be able to do so serenely and with awareness, and for the children about to be born to become agents of blessing in their turn.

# GLOSSARY

NOTE: All terms are Hebrew unless otherwise indicated. In rendering some Hebrew terms into English we have followed the way they are most commonly pronounced, rather than the more strictly grammatical pronunciation.

*Abba*   Father, Daddy.

*achdut*   Oneness.

*Adon Olam*   "Eternal Lord," a prayer sung at the beginning of the Morning Service.

*Adonai*   Lord, a name of God; the Tetragrammaton as pronounced in liturgical settings.

*aggadah*   Legend or mythic lore.

*ahavat ha-Shem*   The love of God.

*Alenu*   Lit. "It is our duty"; concluding prayer of all regular daily, Sabbath, and holiday prayers.

*aliyah*   Lit. "ascension"; emigration to Israel.

*Amidah*   Lit. "standing"; the nineteen-blessing Silent Devotion, centerpiece (with the *Shema* in the morning and evening) of daily prayer services.

*Ari*   Lit. "lion"; acronym for *Adonenu* (our Master) Rabbi Yitzchak: Isaac Luria (1534–1572), leader of a Kabbalist circle in the town of Safed in Israel.

*asiyah*   The world of physical action, lowest of the Four Worlds envisioned by the Kabbalists.

*atzilut*   The world of pure emanation, the highest of the Four Worlds envisioned by the Kabbalists.

*avodah zarah*   Lit. "alien service, alien worship"; idol worship.

*avodat ha-Shem*   Service to God.

*Baal Shem Tov*   Founder of Hasidism (c. 1700–1760). Often shortened to Baal Shem or Besh"t, an acronym.

*bal tashchit*   Lit. "[do] not destroy"; a rabbinic law forbidding pointless destruction, derived from the Torah prohibition against destroying the fruit trees of a city under siege.

*barukh attah Adonai*   "Blessed are you, God," the traditional opening words of Jewish blessings.

*bet midrash*   House of study.

*Birkot ha-Shachar*   Morning blessings.

*bocher*   Youth, student.

*b'rakhah*   Blessing.

*b'riah*   The world of creation, second highest of the Four Worlds envisioned by the Kabbalists.

*bris* (Yid.), *b'rit* (Heb.)   Lit. "covenant"; ritual circumcision.

*bronfen* (Yid.)   Strong drink.

*b'samim*   Fragrant spices, such as cloves, used in the *Havdalah* ceremony.

*Bubbeh* (Yid.)   Grandmother.

*Chabad*   The Hasidic dynasty established by Rabbi Schneur Zalman of Liadi (1745–1812).

*challah*   Braided bread traditionally eaten on the Sabbath and holidays.

*chametz*   Leavening; food made of leavened grains, forbidden in Jewish homes on Passover.

*chesed*   Kindness; piety.

*cheshbon nefesh*   Lit. "keeping the soul's accounts"; reviewing one's personal behavior; examination of conscience.

*chukim* (sing., *chok*)   Ritual commandments that transcend explanation or logic.

*cohen*   A member of the priestly caste, descendant of Moses' brother Aaron.

*davening* (Yid.)   Liturgy or prayer.

*der Aybishter* (Yid.)   "The Most High," a Yiddish appellation for God.

*devekut*   Cleaving, adhering, or loving closeness to God.

*droshe geshank* (Yid.)   Literally, "gift for the [groom's speech or] homily"; a custom of announcing the present that a guest intends to give the wedding couple.

*edot; eduyot*   "Witnessing" commandments; commemorative rituals.

*El*   A name of God traditionally seen as representing God's power and grace.

*Elohim*   A name of God traditionally seen as emphasizing God's rigor and judgment.

*En-Sof*   Infinite; appellation for the transcendent essence of God, used in Kabbalistic settings.

*eruv*   Common shorthand for *eruv chatzerot,* a simulated wall erected by Orthodox Jews to allow objects to be carried within its boundaries on the Sabbath.

*etrog*   Citron, a large citrus fruit, used in the Sukkot ritual.

*etzot*   Advice, counsel, hints.

*farginnt, farginnen*   Wishes well; well-wishing, open-hearted blessing.

*Gehenna* (Yid.)   Purgatory, from Heb. *Gehinnom,* a valley outside Jerusalem where children were sacrificed in pagan times.

*gemilut chasadim*   A bestowal of human kindness.

*gemilut chesed*   The dispensation or repaying of a kindness.

*gesheften* (Yid.)   Dealings, activities, busy-ness.

glatt kosher   Often used today to mean "very kosher." More formally applied to meat that is free of all taint or blemish and whose kashrut is above question.

*Gottenyu* (Yid.)   A diminutive, intimate name for God.

gut Shabbos (Yid.)   "[Have a] good Sabbath," the traditional Sabbath greeting.

*Haftarah*   Portion from the Prophets read after the reading of the Torah on the Sabbath and holidays.

*halakhah*   Lit., "the way"; the greater body of Jewish law or a single point of that law.

*ha-Shem*   "The Name," used in place of *Adonai* in nonliturgical settings.

*Hasidism*    A devotional movement founded by Israel Baal Shem Tov that emphasized ecstatic prayer and closeness to God over scholarship and intellectualism.

*Havdalah*    Lit. "separation"; the ritual that ends the Sabbath and begins the secular week.

*heter*    Lit. "loosening, untying"; permission under Jewish law.

*Hosha'anot*    From *hosha'na,* "please help" or "please save"; a ceremony of supplications and prayers for agricultural fertility conducted on Sukkot.

*issur*    Lit. "binding"; prohibition under Jewish law.

*Kabbalah*    The mystic or esoteric tradition and teachings of Judaism.

*kaddosh*    Holy; set aside or devoted to sacred purpose.

kashrut    The state of kosherness or practice of keeping kosher.

*kavanah*    Lit. "aim"; focus or devotion, intention, mindfulness or attention to prayer, thought, or deed.

*kavanot*    Recommended mental focal points or mind-sets designed to increase *kavanah.*

*kiddush*    Blessing over wine said on Sabbath and holidays.

*kinnuyim*    Epithets or appellations celebrating different attributes of God.

*kishkes* (Yid.)    Insides, internal organs.

*le-dorotam*    Lit. "for their generations," a phrase emphasizing the transmission of tradition to future generations.

*lekach*    Honey cake.

*le-kaddesh*    To sanctify or make holy; to set aside for special purpose.

*lishmor*    To guard or keep.

*Lubavitch*    The active lineage of Chabad Hasidism, named for the town of Rebbe Dov Baer of Lubavitch, second leader of the Chabad lineage.

*lulav*    A palm frond lashed together with shorter branches of the willow and the leafy myrtle tree, used in the Sukkot ritual.

*Ma'ariv*    Evening service.

*Mashiach*    Lit. "anointed one." The Messiah. Also used in Torah to describe priests and kings, who were anointed with oil.

*mashpia*   Spiritual director in Hasidic circles.

*matzah*   Unleavened bread, traditionally eaten during Passover.

*mechitzah*   Partition between the men's and women's sections in Orthodox synagogues.

*melakhah*   Labor; activity traditionally forbidden on the Sabbath.

*melaveh malkah*   Lit. "escorting of the queen"; a Saturday night celebration traditionally held in Hasidic communities after the Sabbath is over.

*melekh ha-olam*   "King of the world [or universe]" the most common form of address for God in most traditional Jewish blessings.

*mensch* (Yid.)   A person who acts decently and fairly to those around him or her; an upstanding member of the community.

*menschlichkeit* (Yid.)   The quality or practice of being a mensch; human decency.

*meshuggeh, meshuggeneh* (Yid.)   Crazy; crazy person.

*mezuzah*   Small roll of parchment containing passages from Deuteronomy and affixed to the doorposts in Jewish houses.

*midrash*   Lit. "seeking out, inquiry"; imaginative and ongoing elucidation of the legal, moral, or spiritual meaning of sacred texts, often in story form.

*mikveh*   Ritual immersion bath.

*Minchah*   Afternoon service.

*minyan*   Minimal prayer quorum, traditionally ten men; prayer group.

*mishkan*   Lit. "sanctuary"; the Tabernacle erected by the Israelites in the desert to house the sacred tablets before the building of the Temple in Jerusalem.

*Mishnah*   Codification of Oral Law.

*mishpatim*   Ethical commandments relating to morality or justice.

*mitzvah*, pl. *mitzvot*   Commandment; good deed.

*mizrach*   East, the direction (Lit. "Orient-ation") in which most Jews in the Diaspora pray so as to face Jerusalem.

*Modeh Ani*   "I thank you," the prayer recited upon waking in the morning.

*mohel*   Circumciser.

*Musaf*   Additional service recited after *Shacharit* on Sabbath and holidays.

*musar*   Morals or ethics; a movement within Judaism that emphasized ethical behavior.

*nefesh*   Breath, breath of life; soul. In the *Sefer Yetzirah,* the realm of the spirit.

*Ne'ilah*   The closing prayer of Yom Kippur.

*neshamah*   Lit. "breath," particularly the out-breath; soul.

*neshamah yeterah*   Additional or superabundance of soul that we receive on Shabbat.

*niggun*   Wordless tune, favored in Hasidic circles.

*Ninth of Av*   Fast day mourning the destruction of the Temple.

*nusach*   Version of traditional prayers used in a given community.

*olam*   Lit. "world"; in the *Sefer Yetzirah,* the physical world.

*Oneg Shabbat*   Lit. "Sabbath joy"; Sabbath party, often held on Saturday afternoon.

*partzufim*   Lit. "masks, faces"; core or archetypal images or names of God.

Pesach   Passover.

*Pesukei de-Zimra*   Lit. "tuneful verses"; part of the morning service.

*Purim*   A festival celebrating the defeat, by Mordecai and Queen Esther, of Haman's plot to destroy the Jews in the days of King Ahasuerus, as described in the Book of Esther.

*rebbe*   Spiritual leader of a Hasidic community.

*Ribboyno shel oylom* (Yid.)   "Master of the Universe," an appellation for God.

*Rosh ha-Shanah*   The Jewish New Year.

*saltz* (Yid.)   Salt.

*sandek* (Yid.)   Godfather, one who holds the baby upon his knees during circumcision.

*schmaltz* (Yid.)   Lit. "animal fat"; sentimentality or camp.

*Seder*   Lit. "order"; the traditional Passover meal.

*sefer Torah*   A Torah scroll.

*Sefer Yetzirah*   The *Book of Creation,* an early Kabbalistic work.

*sefirot*   Spheres or aspects of God.

*Sephardim*   Jews of Spanish and Portuguese descent; used more loosely to include the *edot ha-mizrach,* or "congregations of the East": the Jews of the Arab countries, Greece, Turkey, etc.

*Shabbos* (Yid.), *Shabbat* (Heb.)   Sabbath.

*Shabbosdik* (Yid.)   "Shabbos-like"; fitting or seemly on the Sabbath.

*Shacharit*   Morning service.

*shaleshudes* (Yid.)   The third of the three meals traditionally eaten on the Sabbath.

*shamor*   Guard, keep.

*shanah*   Lit. "year"; in the *Sefer Yetzirah,* the realm of time.

*she-hechiyanu*   A blessing that thanks God for sustaining us to see this day, traditionally said for an event that hasn't happened for at least a year.

*Shekhinah*   The Divine Presence. Often seen as the feminine face of God.

*Shema*   Lit. "hear"; the centerpiece (with the *Amidah*) of morning and evening prayer services, consisting of three passages from the Torah and introduced by the phrase "Hear O Israel, the Lord Our God, the Lord is One."

*shiva* (Yid.), *shiv'ah* (Heb.)   The seven-day period of mourning observed after the death of a close relative.

*shlep* (Yid.)   Drag, carry with effort.

*shmutz* (Yid.)   Dirt, lint.

shofar   Ram's horn.

*sh'virat ha-kelim*   The shattering of vessels that, in Lurianic Kabbalah, accompanied Creation.

*siddur*   Lit. "ordering, arrangement"; the daily prayer book.

*Simchat Torah*   Holiday celebrating the completing of the annual cycle of Torah reading.

*sukkah*   Booth with temporary walls and roofing of branches, used for eating and, in some families, sleeping during the holiday of Sukkot.

*Sukkot*   The Feast of Tabernacles.

*Tachanun*   Penitential section of the weekday Morning Service.

*tallis* (Yid.)    Prayer shawl.

*Talmud*    Compilation of the Mishnah or oral law and the rabbinical discussions of it that were conducted in the first centuries C.E.

*talmud torah*    The teaching and study of sacred texts.

*Tashlikh*    Lit. "casting away"; ceremony on the afternoon of Rosh ha-Shanah in which Jews go to a body of water to symbolically cast away their sins.

*t'chiyat ha-metim*    The resurrection of the dead at the end of days.

*tefillin*    Black leather boxes containing sections of Scripture that are strapped to the arm and head during the weekday morning service.

*tehillim*    Psalms.

*tikkun olam*    The repairing of the world; in Lurianic Kabbalah, the ingathering of light and reversal of the shattering of vessels that accompanied creation.

*tish* (Yid.)    Hasidic term for a sacred gathering around the table.

*trafe* (Yid.)    Lit. "torn," as prey by a predator; now applied to any unkosher food.

*t'shuvah*    Repentance.

*Tu bi-Sh'vat*    The fifteenth of the month of *Shevat,* celebrated as the New Year of the Trees.

*tzaddik*    Saintly or righteous person. In the Hasidic movement, a model figure.

*tzaddik gamur*    A complete *tzaddik,* a perfectly righteous person.

*tz'dakah*    Lit. "justice, righteousness"; the act of giving money to the poor; alms.

*tzitzit* (Heb.), tzitzis (Yid.)    The knotted tassels that appear at each corner of the tallis (prayer shawl) and four-cornered garment traditionally worn under the clothes.

*tzores* (Yid.)    Troubles.

*tz'ror ha-chayim*    Chain of life.

*Yah*    A name of God.

*yahrzeit* (Yid.)    Anniversary of a close relative's death.

*yechidus* (Yid.), *yechidut* (Heb.)   Union; oneness, uniqueness; a hasid's one-on-one meeting with his master in spiritual intimacy.

*yetzirah*   The world of formation, second-lowest of the Four Worlds envisioned by the Kabbalists.

*YHVH*   The Tetragrammaton or unpronounceable name of God.

*yichud*   Unification.

*Yom Kippur*   The Day of Atonement.

*Zaida* (Yid.)   Grandfather.

*zakhor*   Remember.

*Zohar*   A mystical commentary on Torah; the central work of Kabbalah.

# ACKNOWLEDGMENTS

This book has gone through several incarnations, from "What time is it in Paradise?" and "The life that brought me from Restoration to Renewal" to a working theme of "If we are so universalistic, why be Jewish?"

From reams and reams of manuscripts and hours of interviews and phone conversations in my often convoluted and idiosyncratic language, Joel Segel has midwifed, shaped, and birthed a clear and well readable book. I am grateful to him for his word artistry and editorial skill and, most of all, for the way he has successfully brought the reader's perspective to the writing. My sense is that we both have in this way served the Spirit that has deployed us to present this approach to our sacred tradition's current incarnation. Each path and lineage need to be supported by a vivid and energizing dream. Our three thousand years of "God wrestling" are here offered as a postdenominational, posttriumphalist way that honors other sister faiths as part of an organismic cosmology. We hope our book will be part of the means that are now arising for healing our ailing planet.

My family has been supportive of my work, and I am grateful to my wife and partner, Eve Rochelle Ilsen, who has read and critiqued my mind-sketches, and to my children, Miriam, Shalom, Josef, Akiba, Tina, Jon, Alisa, Shalvi, Barya, and Yotam.

I am grateful, too, to my spiritual children, colleagues, and friends, all soul relatives with whom I have shared some of these thoughts: Rabbis Shimon Brand, Bahir Davis, Tirzah Firestone, Mordechai Gafni, Elliott Ginsberg, Arthur Green, Julie Greenberg, Nadia Gross, Victor Gross, Shaya Isenberg, Ruth Kagan, Miles Krassen, Leah Novick, Nehemia Polen, Marcia Prager, Daniel Siegel, Moshe Waldoks, and Gershon Winkler; also Barkan (Barry) Alter, Mark Gerzon, Avrum Goodblatt, Amy Hertz, Betty Hilton, Ivan Itzkovics, Dr. Michael Kagan, Rodger Kamenetz, Susan Saxe, Ruth Seagull, M. Singer, Jocelyn Wilson, and Nathaniel Yepez.

Thanks also to Aleph, Elat Chayyim, the Kallah, Naropa University, the Nathan Cummings Foundation, Ohalah, the Righteous Persons Foundation, and the Spiritual Eldering Institute. The Yesod Foundation for a Jewish Future initiated the writing of this book through a seed grant and is now, with Naropa University, engaged in gathering and preserving my archives.

I know that as I am reaching my eightieth birthday, I may have in one of my "senior moments" forgotten to put your name on this list. If you feel this, please consider yourself included.

—Z. S. S.

Thanks to: Reb Zalman, for his deep roots and exuberant branches; for bringing life, love, and vision to our people; for extending his faith and blessing to this *misnagged;* for showing me how to talk to God; and for the way he ties his shoes. Amy Hertz, for lightness of spirit and clarity of vision. Cindy Spiegel, for her patient encouragement and care. Marc Haeringer and Susan Ambler, for smoothing the way. Mama Eve

Ilsen, for warmth and hospitality. Yotam, for intelligent conversation and a spare comb. Jonathan D. Stoler, who opened his home to a stranger. Bill Novak, for sage counsel and encouragement all the way down the line. Peter Turner and Sam Bercholz at Shambhala, for their understanding. Mordechai Liebling and Moshe Waldoks, for Zalman lore. Ruth Budner, Diane Freedman, Myra MacCuaig and her family, Mitch Rosenberg, Laura Segel, Daniel Siegel, Ken Sipser, Dan Soyer, Jonathan Stoler, Chris Taranta and his study group, and Rob Woods, for their warm and constructive comments on this manuscript.

Thanks to Mel Brown and the rest of my study mates of Ten Men and at Beth El in Sudbury, Massachusetts, and to Avi and Amir Ziv, my traveling companions on the A train. To Laura Segel, for her love and trust, for rejoicing in my rejoicing and picking up the slack so I could get more work done. To Eve and Jesse Segel, my beautiful children: may God bless and keep you always. To my parents, for sowing the seeds and tending them with love and forbearance. To Myer Galinski, for passing on the stories. To Minna Margolis Segel, whose light still shines.

*Ma ashiv la-Adonai, kol tagmulohi alai* (Psalms 116:12). What can I give back to God, whose every blessing is upon me?

—J. J. S.